HKCER PAPERBACKS

Already Published

Towards Open Skies and Uncongested Airports: An Opportunity for Hong Kong
by Kai-Sun Kwong

Market Environmentalism: Lessons for Hong Kong
by Jo Ann Kwong

Friedman in China
by Milton Friedman

International Telecommunications in Hong Kong: The Case for Liberalization
by Milton Mueller

Economic Reform in China: Analyses, Reflections, and Prospects
edited by Dianqing Xu, Francis T. M. Lui, and Hsin Zhang

Health Care in Hong Kong: An Economic Policy Assessment
by Joel W. Hay

A Friedman Lecture Fund Monograph

AIR CARGO AND THE OPENING OF CHINA

The Hong Kong Centre for Economic Research

The Centre was set up as a research and educational trust under a trust deed signed in 1987. It supports research and publishes studies on public policy issues to promote understanding of economic affairs and provide alternative policy choices.

The Centre's work is assisted by an international board of advisers:

The Centre is an approved tax-exempted charitable trust controlled by Trustees and financed by sales of publications and voluntary contributions from individuals, organizations and companies.

Richard Y. C. Wong, Director

The Hong Kong Centre for Economic Research
School of Economics and Finance
The University of Hong Kong
Pokfulam Road, Hong Kong
Tel: 5478313 Fax:852-5486319

A Friedman Lecture Fund Monograph

Air Cargo and the Opening of China

New Opportunities for Hong Kong

Joseph P. Schwieterman

Published for

The Hong Kong Centre for Economic Research

by

The Chinese University Press

ISBN 962–201–612–X

THE CHINESE UNIVERSITY PRESS
The Chinese University of Hong Kong
SHATIN, N. T., HONG KONG

Printed in Hong Kong by Nam Fung Printing Co., Ltd.

The Friedman Lecture Fund was established from proceeds obtained from a public lecture given by Dr. Milton Friedman on 24 September 1988 in Hong Kong. The purpose of the Fund is to support research that leads to an improved understanding of the role of markets in economic life. To this end the Fund supports the work of individual scholars and institutions. The Fund is operated jointly by the Hong Kong Centre for Economic Research and the School of Economics and Finance of the University of Hong Kong.

The Friedman Lecture Fund was established from proceeds obtained from a public lecture given by Dr. Milton Friedman on 24 September 1998 in Hong Kong. The purpose of the Fund is to support research that leads to an improved understanding of the role of markets in economic life. To this end the Fund supports the work of individual scholars and institutions. The Fund is operated jointly by the Hong Kong Centre for Economic Research and the School of Economics and Finance of the University of Hong Kong.

Contents

Foreword

The HKCER Paperbacks are planned to be studies of medium length in which economists would analyse a policy issue from an economic perspective. Authors are invited, in particular, to consider the circumstances which encouraged or inhibited the translation of ideas into policy.

The opening of China in the 1980s has created vast opportunities for Hong Kong manufacturers to invest in export-oriented outward processing activities across the border. This has transformed Hong Kong from an export driven manufacturing centre into an entrepôt and service economy. Today, Hong Kong firms employ more workers in China than the entire labour force of Hong Kong and account for nearly two-thirds of all foreign investments in China. Since half of the total exports of China are shipped through Hong Kong, the demand for shipping, both by sea and by air, and other related services have grown rapidly. The physical infrastructure comprising road networks, container terminals and air cargo terminals have come under increasing capacity constraints. The problem is particularly acute in air shipping services because Kai Tak Airport will become saturated well before the new airport at Chek Lap Kok can come into operation. In 1992, Hong Kong imported HK$958 billion and exported HK$925 billion worth of merchandise, of which 17.8 percent of imports and 17.8 percent of export were shipped by air.

This study by Dr. Joseph Schwieterman shows that capacity limits due to physical infrastructure is not the only factor that is hampering the ability of Hong Kong entrepreneurs to respond to the new economic opportunities. He argues that the present practice of awarding a monopoly franchise in air cargo terminal services and the regulatory restrictions imposed by air freight service agreements severely limits the scope for competition. This results in higher prices on air freight services and less choice for the customer. If Hong Kong is to develop into an Asian air cargo hub, these regulatory constraints would have to be liberalized.

In the area of air cargo terminal services, Dr. Schwieterman urges the Provisional Airport Authority to (1) award licenses to two or more independent terminal operators in the new Chek Lap Kok airport, (2) select at least one company to operate a terminal that offers a separate dedicated area for express cargo, (3) allow terminal operators complete freedom in pricing and encourage competition to eliminate the need for regulation of prices or profits, and (4) charge each operator an annual franchise fee proportional to its use of airport land and choose operators on the strength of their proposals. He cites the successful example of Singapore's Changi Airport on the workability of competition under a two-terminal system without price and profit regulations.

The study also proposes to remove all-cargo flights from bilateral service agreements. Hong Kong should unilaterally offer fifth freedom rights for a limited number of all-cargo flights between Hong Kong and other major Asian destinations. This according to the author would demonstrate Hong Kong's commitment to becoming a viable hub candidate in the Asian region and forestall the development of competing hubs at a time when Hong Kong would be plagued by capacity constraints. Dr. Schwieterman also urges Hong Kong to provide unrestricted access for all-cargo flights serving Chek Lap Kok and to authorize a second local carrier to provide all-cargo services to important destinations where permitted by bilateral treaties.

The author argues that as one of the fastest growing economies in the world, south China should be served by a dynamic and responsive air cargo industry. In the words of the author, Hong Kong cannot afford to stand idly by and place the future of Chek Lap Kok in the hands of a single terminal operator or trust it to an unwieldy and unresponsive bilateral negotiating process. The construction of Chek Lap Kok airport has been delayed by complex negotiations involving the Chinese and British governments whose agendas have from time to time been dominated by problems associated with the transfer of sovereignty over Hong Kong in 1997. It would be an even greater tragedy if at the end of day when Hong Kong has the new airport its value is diminished by regulatory constraints that fail to promote competition.

The Trustees, Advisers and Director of the Hong Kong Centre for Economic Research, must formally dissociate themselves from the conclusions of the Paperback, while welcoming its timely contribution to a major issue in Hong Kong.

Richard Y. C. Wong
July 1993

tragedy if at the end of day when Hong Kong has the new airport its value is diminished by regulatory constraints that fail to promote competition.

The Trustees, Advisers and Director of the Hong Kong Centre for Economic Research must formally dissociate themselves from the conclusions of the Papers, while welcoming its timely contribution to a major issue in Hong Kong.

Richard Y. C. Wong
July 1995

The Author

Dr. Joseph P. Schwieterman is an assistant professor in the Management of Public Services Program at DePaul University, located in Chicago, Illinois. He received his Ph.D. in public policy studies at the University of Chicago, a master's degree in transportation policy from Northwestern University, and his B.S. in management from Purdue University. Dr. Schwieterman is a specialist in transportation economics and the analysis of infrastructure projects. His articles appear in the *Journal of the Transportation Research Forum*, *Regulation, Transportation Research Record*, and a recently published book by the American Enterprise Institute. Various magazines and newspapers such as the *New York Times, USA Today*, and the *Detroit News* also have covered his research.

Dr. Schwieterman has extensive experience as a professional in the transportation industry. He worked for eight years as a research analyst with United Airlines, evaluating pricing and economic issues, and is a member of the Aviation Economics and Forecasting Committee of the Transportation Research Board.

Acknowledgements

Few places can match the stimulating environment of Hong Kong for the study of international transportation issues. The willingness of local officials to share data, anecdotes, and opinions testifies to Hong Kong's bright future as a center for Asian commerce.

I gratefully acknowledge the support of the Hong Kong Centre for Economic Research which made this project possible. Special thanks are due to Centre members Richard Y.C. Wong, Alan K.F. Siu and Eliza Chan. I would also like to thank those who generously shared their views, including P.T. Bangsberg, Phillip Bowring, Anthony Charter, Gilbert Chow, Po Chung, Julia Hui Ching Ling, Donald Curran, Roy Delbyck, Richard Golasewski, Chan Wing Kee, Andrew Herdman, Anthony Interlandy, Norman Miners, Tony Norman, Martin Savery, David Shoenfeld, Melody Townsel, Michael Westlake, Chan Wai-kwan, Clement Yeung, Sung Yun-Wing, two anonymous referees, and many others. Finally, I thank Karen MacLeod and Cheri White for their editorial assistance.

The views expressed here are solely those of the author.

Executive Summary

Hong Kong is in the midst of critical decision-making regarding air cargo services. These decisions will affect Hong Kong's ability to effectively use its new airport at Chek Lap Kok and to meet the transportation demands of the South China region. This study shows that Hong Kong must take two steps to foster regional economic growth:

- The Provisional Airport Authority (PAA) must provide a dynamic and competitive market for terminal services at Chek Lap Kok.
- The Economic Services Branch must remove all-cargo ("freighter") flights from the cumbersome bilateral process that is restricting innovation, risk taking, and expansion.

Taking these steps would yield tremendous payoffs. Not only would it assure the availability of low-cost air cargo service throughout Hong Kong and Guangdong Province, it would also pave the way toward Chek Lap Kok's development as a major cargo hub, producing more than HK$4 billion in regional benefits. Taking these steps would help the region meet the exploding market for "express" services that move small parcels, packages, and other time-sensitive merchandise. The two initiatives would also improve the new airport's financial position and give Hong Kong the resources to meet the 700 percent growth in regional air cargo tonnage which is anticipated by 2030.

Express services are expanding by 25 percent annually throughout the Pacific Rim and doubling each year in Guangdong Province. Carriers of express cargo, already the dominant providers of air freight service in Europe and North America, are expanding rapidly to meet this rising regional demand: Federal Express is experimenting with a connecting complex in Taipei; TNT Express Worldwide is operating a mini-hub in Manila; DHL International, Inc. is investing in terminals and express centers throughout the region;

and United Parcel Service is purchasing new, widebody aircraft to abet its Asian expansion. Through coordinated night-time flight connections at a hub, carriers soon will be able to collect cargo each evening and guarantee its delivery to any major Asia–Pacific destination the following morning. Hong Kong, Taipei, Manila, Shenzhen, Singapore and other cities are competing to become the region's dominant express hub. Hong Kong has geographic and commercial advantages over the other sites. However, Hong Kong has not yet committed itself to taking the actions necessary to make a major express hub viable, and thus risks losing the contest.

It is estimated that the creation of an express cargo hub at Chek Lap Kok will yield HK$329 million to HK$591 million annually by enhancing competition and providing substantial new revenues for the future Airport Authority. A hub would also improve service quality by providing more attractive "close out" times (i.e., terminal deadlines) and by offering new non-stop flights to regional destinations. In addition, the hub would help lower terminal rates and give shippers access to an advanced electronic data interface (EDI) system.

A vital step toward hub development at Chek Lap Kok is providing a competitive market for terminal services. Before the middle of 1994, the Provisional Airport Authority must decide on the number of cargo terminal licenses it will award. Five companies have submitted proposals to build and operate terminals. Currently, Hong Kong Air Cargo Terminals Limited (HACTL) owns and operates all cargo terminal facilities at Hong Kong International Airport (Kai Tak) under an exclusive license with the Hong Kong government. (Its profits are limited, by government regulation, to 12.05 percent of its assets.) An extension of this type of monopoly arrangement would undermine Chek Lap Kok's development as a major express hub. Local policymakers must understand that none of the world's 10 largest express cargo hubs are located at airports where a monopoly terminal prevails.

The study urges the Provisional Airport Authority to take action on four initiatives:

- Award licenses to two independent terminal operators (or three operators if additional space can be made available for cargo terminals) with each terminal operator authorized to handle both express and general cargo.

- Select at least one company affiliated with an express carrier to operate a terminal that offers a separate, dedicated area for express cargo.
- Allow terminal operators complete freedom in pricing, encouraging competition to eliminate the need for regulation of prices or profits.
- Charge each terminal operator a flat, annual franchise fee proportional to its use of airport land and choose operators on the strength of their proposals, thus avoiding an "open tender" bidding system.

This approach offers many advantages. It would provide terminal operators with the impetus to meet the growing demand for specialized terminal services, including "matrix" sorting systems, computer scanners, and automated conveyor systems. It would encourage operators to lease out terminal space and authorize carriers to develop their own on-site operating procedures and freight warehousing. In addition, it would enhance opportunities for contingency planning, allowing airlines to alter their procedures in the event of bad weather, mechanical problems, or schedule irregularities. Finally, it would insulate carriers from many of the political uncertainties associated with reunification, adding stability to their investments in the turbulent Hong Kong marketplace. The proposal allowing express carriers to directly own and operate a terminal would further encourage efficient terminal design and management. Many other Asian cities, including Manila, Shenzhen, Seoul, and Singapore, have already taken steps to award carriers this right.

By effectively guaranteeing profits, the current monopoly arrangement dampens the terminal operator's incentive to introduce new services. The operator is given little impetus to respond quickly to carriers' requests for non-conventional services or to give carriers the authority to intervene in the quality control process. This renders air cargo services more susceptible to communication breakdowns, disputes, and delays.

Not everyone agrees that competitive terminals are best for the region. Supporters of a continued monopoly contend that a single operator is necessary to enhance the efficiency of terminal operations through economies of scale. This argument considers terminal services to be a featureless commodity with little need for product differentiation. Such a stance is inconsistent with situations in airports throughout Europe and North America, where carriers are willing to pay substantial premiums for a terminal operator's specialized services.

Advocates of a single operator also contend that this arrangement is necessary to allow freight forwarders and trucking companies to continue interacting with only one entity. This argument underestimates the adaptability of these institutions. Facing competition from express carriers, for example, local forwarders are proving to be dynamic and resilient, rapidly improving their services and marketing sophistication. For the first time, many forwarders are providing door-to-door and global sourcing services. Shippers would have been denied these improvements had forwarders been protected from change.

A two-terminal system may not provide the same level of price competition as a multi-terminal system. It is unfortunate that only two (or possibly three) terminals can be situated on the 22-hectare Chek Lap Kok cargo site because of the lack of space. However, a stable cartel is not likely to develop. Cartels tend to be unstable when members have opportunities to expand their output at the expense of other cartel members. While terminal operators do not have this opportunity at Kwai Chung container port because of its chronic capacity shortages, ample capacity will be available at Chek Lap Kok. A small loss in market share could mean a significant loss in profits for a terminal operator. A cartel would also be destabilized by new regional airports in Shenzhen, Macao, and Guangzhou, which would afford carriers considerable leverage in negotiating favorable rates. Authorizing express carriers to operate a facility would further lessen the risk of a cartel as these carriers are "newcomers" to the regional terminal scene.

The Airport Authority could, as a last resort, re-establish a "scheme of control" to keep profits at competitive levels if a stable cartel were to develop. However, the regulatory path is a poor substitute for competition. Although it keeps prices at bay, regulation dampens incentives for innovation and efficiency. Price regulation also is susceptible to misuse and can become a tool to keep prices high, a legal mechanism enforcing a cartel's price.

Singapore's Changi Airport illustrates the workability of competition under a two-terminal system. Both terminal operators, Singapore Air Terminal Services (SATS) and Changi International Airport Services (CIAS), are making profits and expanding. Shippers have been so satisfied with the unregulated duopoly arrangement that they consistently rank both operators as among the top three in Asia.

This study calls for the Provisional Airport Authority to choose terminal operators on the basis of the merits of their design and financial plan. Such a practice offers significant advantages over the "open tender" scheme sometimes used to award terminal licenses at Kwai Chung. An open tender bidding system would favor those operators that expect to earn monopoly profits through market domination. Any additional revenues earned by the PAA through this system would not be real benefits to the local economy, but merely transfers from shippers and consumers to the government, financed by higher terminal rates.

The call for a competitive market for terminal service is not an indictment against HACTL. The company deserves serious consideration for a Chek Lap Kok license. However, considering the rapid pace of innovation and the competition from other Asian airports, Hong Kong must enlist the services of several operators to retain its position as a preeminent cargo center.

Terminals are not the only problem facing the local cargo industry. For Chek Lap Kok to reach its potential as a cargo hub, cargo services must be freed from the cumbersome bilateral negotiating process that is hampering innovation and expansion. At present, the Hong Kong government negotiates with foreign governments for various air service "freedoms" on behalf of passenger and cargo airlines, following the precedent established by the 1946 "Bermuda I" conference. The outcomes of this bilateral process are air service agreements that control foreign carriers' access into Hong Kong, as well as these carriers' flight capacities.

This regulatory system is being used to protect the market share of local carriers, such as Cathay Pacific Airlines. Attempts by foreign governments to negotiate fifth freedom rights (i.e., the right for an airline to fly between Hong Kong and another foreign country) for cargo airlines systematically fail. Hong Kong's unyielding position on this and other bargaining issues leaves little room for compromise. Considering that negotiations will continue to be dominated by complex passenger-related issues, progress at the bargaining table is unlikely anytime soon. This is damaging to the regional economy. It is increasing air cargo prices by 5 percent, costing shippers HK$700 million annually. It is suppressing innovation and exposing shippers regionwide to the risk of foreign government retaliation.

Governments worldwide are freeing their air cargo industries from these types of restrictive bilateral treaties. Neighboring countries, such as the Philippines, Singapore, South Korea, and Taiwan offer many foreign carriers virtually unrestricted access to their airports. Greece, Italy, Spain, and the United States have taken steps to remove cargo services from bilateral treaties governing passenger services; the European Community recently gave the airlines of its member states unlimited authority to carry both cargo and passenger between any two points within the Community's borders. In this environment, Hong Kong's defensive and unyielding position on some of its bilateral negotiations has rightfully earned the territory a reputation as a militant adversary of free trade in air cargo services.

The study proposes a series of initiatives to remove all-cargo flights from bilateral control:

- Unilaterally offer fifth freedom rights for a limited number of all-cargo flights (five to ten daily) between Kai Tak Airport and other major Asian destinations. This step would demonstrate Hong Kong's commitment to becoming a viable hub candidate and would allow potential hub operators to gain a stronger foothold in the South China market. (A competitive bidding system would be used if several carriers simultaneously requested these new traffic rights.)
- Provide unrestricted access for all-cargo flights serving Chek Lap Kok. This would enhance hub opportunities at the new airport and allow carriers to confidently prepare for future expansion.

- Authorize a second local carrier to provide all-cargo services to important destinations where permitted by bilateral treaties. The Air Transport Licensing Authority's existing policy generally allows only one Hong Kong based carrier per route, denying local carriers access to important cargo markets. Air Hong Kong appears to be an eager candidate to launch scheduled service between Hong Kong and Los Angeles, Seoul, Taipei, and Tokyo.
- Give new entrants the ability to expand by designating some of the additional capacity that will become available at Kai Tak Airport in 1994 to all-cargo flights serving major Asian destinations.

The above proposals are limited to all-cargo flights for reasons of political expediency. Considering the complex diplomatic issues pertaining to passenger services, the unwieldy bilateral process for passenger flights is unlikely to be overhauled in the near future. However, because "belly" cargo services provided in conjunction with passenger flights need to expand, Hong Kong is urged to support efforts to remove belly services from the bilateral process as well. It should support a multilateral negotiating process, such as the General Agreement on Tariffs and Trade (GATT), for all types of cargo service. Already, countries in Europe, Southeast Asia, and South America are moving in this direction.

As one of the world's fastest growing economies, South China needs a dynamic and responsive air cargo industry. The region cannot afford to stand idly by and place the future of Chek Lap Kok in the hands of a single terminal operator or trust it to an unwieldy and unresponsive negotiating process. The above-outlined policy choices would sweep away the outmoded, anti-competitive policies that are inhibiting regional growth and pave the way toward a vital and prosperous Chek Lap Kok enterprise.

Chapter 1

Air Cargo and the Opening of China

Hong Kong will be able to effectively use its new airport at Chek Lap Kok and meet growing transportation demands in the South China region only if the air cargo industry has enough flexibility to expand and diversify. This study outlines steps Hong Kong must take to enhance Chek Lap Kok's role as a facilitator of regional economic growth. A competitive market for terminal service at Chek Lap Kok, the removal of all-cargo flights from restrictive air service agreements, and new expansion opportunities for local cargo airlines are essential to the region's growth and prosperity.

At stake is not only the availability of low-cost air cargo service throughout Hong Kong and Guangdong Province, but more than HK$4 billion worth of benefits associated with the development of Chek Lap Kok as an express cargo hub. A comprehensive hub for Asian cargo at the new airport would vastly improve service quality and enhance the new airport's financial condition. However, Hong Kong has not yet committed itself to making the necessary changes for developing a hub at the airport and risks losing the opportunity to do so.

The study begins by examining the critical elements of Hong Kong's air cargo industry and its expanding role in the South China economy. Chapter 2 examines the potential benefits to the regional economy of Chek Lap Kok's development as a cargo hub. Chapter 3 outlines the steps the Provisional Airport Authority must take to make a competitive market for terminal services a reality at Chek Lap Kok. Chapter 4 and Chapter 5 explore the problems associated with the existing bilateral approach for air cargo regulation and offer practical recommendations to make Chek Lap Kok more accessible to cargo airlines. Unless these changes are made soon, growth-hungry airports elsewhere in Asia will undermine Hong Kong's position as the dominant air cargo center in the region and nullify its chances of improving service and fostering regional growth.

1. Air Cargo Industry Profile

The opening of China and the growth of its market economy is bolstering the demand for transportation services in Hong Kong. Although Hong Kong has a population of only 6 million and an area of only 400 square miles, its oceangoing shipping companies now handle more containers than any other port in the world. Its airlines also dominate the regional air cargo market. Forty-seven airlines and 250 freight forwarders move more than 2,000 tonnes of cargo through Hong Kong International Airport (Kai Tak) daily, making Hong Kong the third busiest air cargo center in the world (IATA, 1991). Hong Kong handles more airborne cargo than Great Britain. Hong Kong's annual commercial "throughput," the total amount of cargo moving through air freight terminals, soon will surpass 1 million tonnes — enough to fill 10,000 jumbo jets.

Air cargo, one of Hong Kong's least studied sectors, has been instrumental in elevating Hong Kong into the world's tenth largest trading entity. More than HK$100 billion in merchandise from more than 700 companies in Hong Kong is shipped via air annually. Local shippers of air cargo account for more than HK$248 billion in annual sales and HK$15 billion in annual payroll, and employ more than a quarter of a million local residents (Gellman, 1990). The industry is equally vital to China's Guangdong Province, where manufacturers now transport as much airborne cargo through Kai Tak as do manufacturers in Hong Kong.

Local shippers of high-value merchandise are most dependent on air cargo services. Measured by weight, air services account for only 1 percent of Hong Kong's total cargo throughput. However, measured in terms of value, air services account for more than 20 percent of the throughput (Linn, 1993). Moreover, total airborne tonnage is growing by more than 10 percent annually, despite a lingering recession that has suppressed air cargo growth worldwide and negatively affected Hong Kong's major trading partners, including Japan, the United States, and Germany.

Few appreciate the vital role that air cargo services play in all four major categories of Hong Kong trade (Table 1.1):

- Domestic exports are goods produced entirely within Hong Kong. In terms of value, 34 percent of all domestic exports are shipped via air. Clothing, office equipment, watches and clocks, photographic equipment, and jewelry dominate this category.

Table 1.1. Major Commodities Shipped by Air – 1992 Estimates

	HK$ in Millions	Annual Growth
Domestic Exports:		
1. Clothing	21,879	–7.6%
2. Office Equipment	11,569	21.2%
3. Watches and Clocks	10,654	–12.2%
4. Photographic Components	6,984	28.8%
5. Jewelry	4,778	–6.2%
6. Data Processing Machines	2,140	63.5%
7. Electrical Switches	2,087	4.2%
All merchandise	*70,173*	*1.4%*
Re-exports:		
1. Clothing	17,097	21.9%
2. Watches and Clocks	11,901	34.6%
3. Photographic Components	11,638	20.2%
4. Jewelry	9,506	–4.2%
5. Office Equipment	5,888	60.2%
6. Telecommunications	3,295	37.6%
7. Travel Goods	3,212	26.6%
All merchandise	*91,795*	*23.9%*
Imports:		
1. Photographic Components	37,852	26.4%
2. Jewelry	21,119	19.0%
3. Watches and Clocks	18,613	6.8%
4. Office Equipment	9,171	25.2%
5. Telecommunications	8,635	26.2%
6. Data Processing Machines	5,855	58.9%
7. Clothing	5,657	19.9%
All merchandise	*170,636*	*22.5%*

Source: *Shippers Today* (1993).

- Re-exports are goods imported by local buyers for improvement through sorting, bottling, packaging, decorating, or other "value-added" processing. In terms of value, 23 percent of all re-exports are shipped via air. The five leading re-export categories are the same as those for domestic exports.
- Imports are goods shipped to Hong Kong for use by its residents or retailers. About 20 percent of imports are shipped via air. Photographic components are by far the largest category, followed by jewelry and watches and clocks.

Transshipped goods are finished goods transported to Hong Kong (and perhaps stored there temporarily) prior to shipment abroad. These goods are not officially considered part of Hong Kong's export trade because they do not clear customs.

The impressive, 20-percent annual growth of imports and re-exports is not attributable to any particular product category. In fact, both imports and re-exports are rising briskly across *all* major product categories except jewelry, which is one of Hong Kong's few sagging re-export sectors. The performance of domestic exports, where growth is being thwarted by the relocation of Hong Kong manufacturers to the mainland, is less impressive. Domestic exports rose by about 1 percent last year, but they fell by more than 7 percent for clothing, Hong Kong's leading domestic export.

The strength of the local air cargo industry lies in its diversified mix of customers. No single destination dominates the export market. Loadings to various Asian destinations account for slightly more than half of commercial throughput, while loadings to North America and Europe cumulatively account for about 40 percent. Nevertheless, the North American and European markets command the most attention, contributing an estimated 80 percent of revenues due to the longer travel distances involved. A typical air cargo shipment to Japan costs about HK$16 per kilogram while a similar shipment to New York costs at least HK$60 per kilogram.

Hong Kong's four largest air cargo export markets, the United States, Japan, Taiwan, and Germany, contribute just over half of the total air cargo throughput (Table 1.2). Exports to growing Asian countries, including Taiwan, South Korea, and Singapore, are growing most rapidly, having expanded in 1992 by more than 20 percent. At the same time, shipments to certain "mature" markets, such as Germany and the Netherlands, are falling. Trade patterns are steadily changing as developing countries, including Cambodia, Laos, Indonesia, The Philippines, and Vietnam, establish themselves as Hong Kong's newest re-export sectors. Although accounting for less than 10 percent of commercial throughput, air cargo shipments to these destinations are rising by more than 25 percent annually.

Carrier Profile

Expansion has not been easy for many industry participants. Under the existing system of bilateral treaties between governments, cargo airlines cannot readily add flights to new destinations in response to changing market conditions. They must conform to governmentally negotiated air service agreements (ASAs), which control frequencies, capacities, and destinations of flights. Air service agreements in Hong Kong are the products of bilateral discussions between foreign governments and are shown in Chapter 4 to adversely affect prices

Table 1.2. Leading Air Cargo Export Markets

Destination	Tonnage	Growth
1. U.S.A.	108,593	16.4%
2. Japan	103,010	7.3%
3. Taiwan	51,965	22.0%
4. Germany	39,231	–3.6%
5. South Korea	31,069	24.7%
6. United Kingdom	28,431	11.4%
7. Singapore	25,371	22.9%
8. Thailand	19,611	0.2%
9. France	18,138	8.6%
10. China	17,823	11.9%
11. Belgium	17,416	26.0%
12. Netherlands	15,476	–6.1%
To all countries	534,286	11.9%

Includes domestic exports and re-exports only (Transhipped goods excluded).
Source: *Shippers Today* (1993).

and operating efficiency in the industry.

Two types of cargo airlines, general cargo carriers and express cargo carriers, are vying to expand in Hong Kong. General cargo carriers specialize in airport-to-airport (ATA) freight, often working in conjunction with ground handlers such as freight forwarders or trucking companies. The majority of general cargo is transported in the "belly" compartments of passenger aircraft. Express carriers, or "integrators," offer higher-priced, specialized services that cater to the more time-sensitive segment of the market. These carriers emphasize highly valued "priority" cargo such as parcels, documents, and packages. Within these classifications are scheduled carriers, which operate on fixed timetables, and charter carriers, which provide more intermittent service, usually emphasizing the busy shipping season extending from late summer through November.

Only one carrier, Cathay Pacific Airlines, commands an appreciable share of the total market. A general cargo carrier based in Hong Kong, Cathay holds a 30-percent market share based on total tonnage (Figure 1.1). China Air, Lufthansa, and Japan Air Lines also are leading participants, but hold shares of 6 percent or less. Federal Express has the largest share among express carriers, while Martinair has the largest share among charter carriers. As these statistics show, locally based carriers such as Cathay and Air Hong Kong handle only about one-third of all cargo while foreign-based airlines handle the remaining two-thirds. Among foreign carriers, those based in Asia are dominant, handling roughly 35 percent of the cargo, while European carriers handle about 18 percent and North American carriers handle about 12 percent.

Most foreign airlines carry belly cargo and are therefore capable of transporting only smaller cargo containers. Two foreign airlines, Swiss Air and KLM Royal Dutch airlines, offer "combination" service on specially partitioned passenger aircraft that can handle several large, twenty-foot container units. Seven foreign airlines — Northwest Airlines, Lufthansa, Air France, Korean Airlines, Japan Air Lines, Nippon Cargo Airlines and China Air — operate scheduled "freighter" services, which carry no passengers. Charter carriers, including Luxembourg-based Cargolux Airlines and Martinair, a

Figure 1.1. Market Share of Cargo Airlines, 1992*

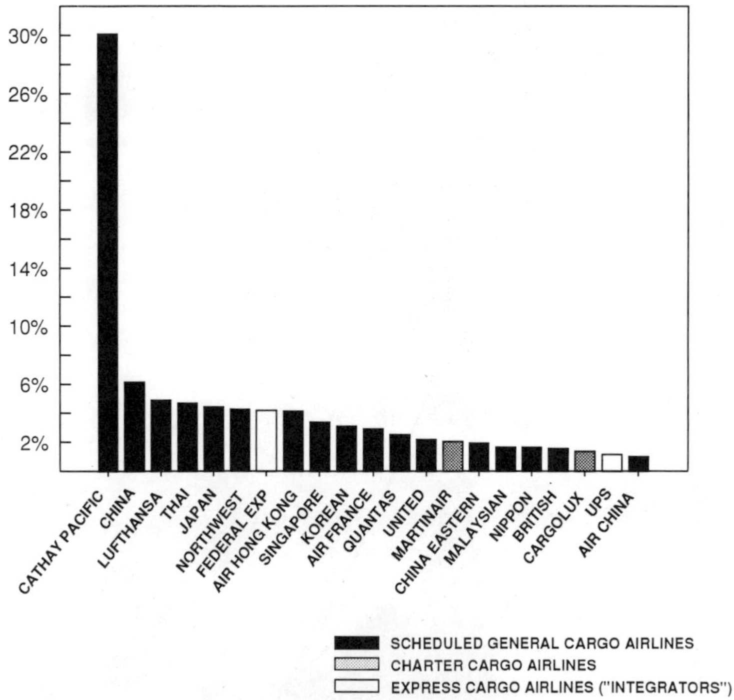

* Estimate based on Nov. 1991 – Nov. 1992 data.
Source: *Hong Kong Air Transport Movements*, Nov. 1992.

Dutch entity, also operate freighters on a seasonal basis to Europe and the U.S.

Altogether, Hong Kong's airlines carry cargo directly to 96 destinations and indirectly to thousands of other destinations through transfers at other airports. Freighters are currently operated to 19 destinations (Figure 1.2). The growing network of all-cargo flights handles about 30 percent of all cargo to and from Hong Kong.

Hong Kong's freight forwarders handle more than 75 percent of the cargo shipped to and from the airport. As the intermediaries between shippers and airlines, forwarders negotiate with airlines for favorable prices and space, arrange for the pickup and delivery of

Figure 1.2. Principal Freighter Routes, 1993

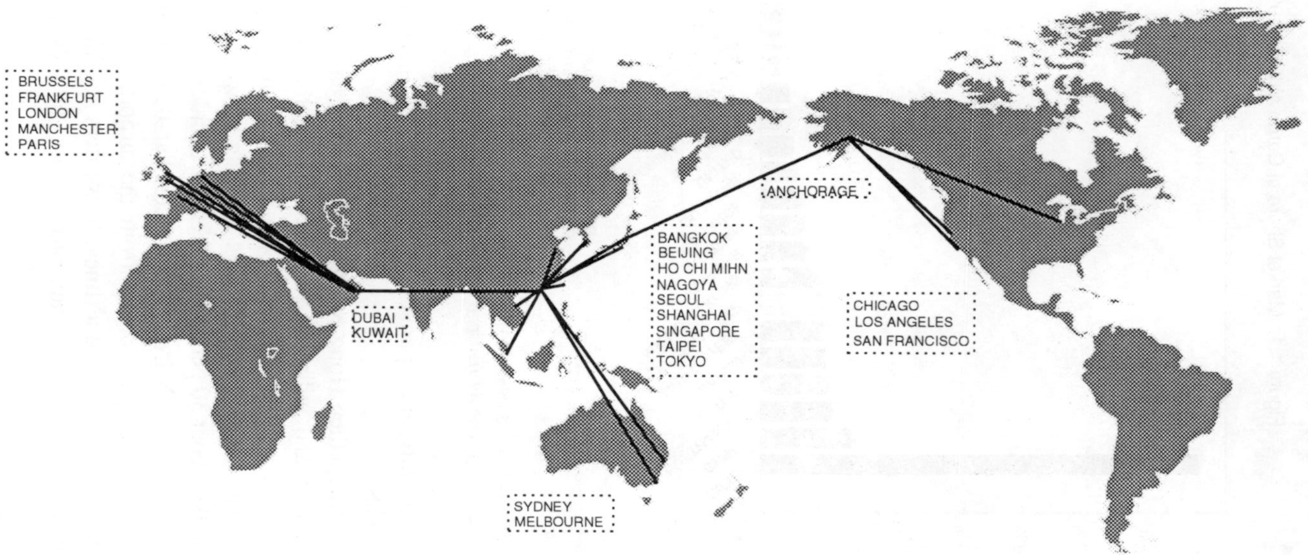

cargo at shippers' facilities, and provide ancillary services such as storage, customs clearance and paperwork processing. Because forwarders are able to consolidate cargo from many customers into large, container-sized shipments, they offer lower rates than shippers could obtain through independent negotiations. More than 250 forwarding companies, many affiliated with international forwarding networks, serve the territory.

2. Air Cargo and the Opening of China's Economy

As China's age-old *entrepôt*, or distribution point for international trade, Hong Kong and its air cargo industry are inextricably linked to the commercial success of the mainland. China's expanding economy was largely responsible for the 15-fold increase in air cargo volume between 1970 and 1991. During the period, commercial throughput rose from 52,000 tonnes to 812,000 tonnes — 75 percent of it consisting of materials or merchandise from the mainland (*Report on Civil Aviation*, 1992). Since 1978, when China's economy was opened to foreign investment, throughput has risen by 250 percent — 25 percentage points higher than passenger traffic to Hong Kong. Cargo volumes grew even in the politically turbulent years following the Tiananman Square incident, which temporarily disrupted the region's economic expansion.

China's manufacturing sector needs Hong Kong's air cargo services to sustain its expanding market economy. Nearly two decades after China began its drive for self-sufficiency, about half of its exports are still being shipped through Hong Kong, and nearly two-thirds of its foreign investments involve Hong Kong corporations. Hong Kong's air cargo services are critical to the thousands of manufacturers on the mainland that are unable to trade directly with overseas buyers due to the high transportation and transactions costs involved (Sung, 1991). A structure consolidating trade through Hong Kong's middlemen and air cargo providers allows the manufacturers to interact with a single agent, reducing the costs associated with arranging and negotiating sales.

The inadequacy of its own airports, which operate on a much

smaller scale and are less efficient technically than those in Hong Kong, heightens the mainland's dependence on Hong Kong's air cargo services. China's progress in improving its infrastructure has been sluggish, making the development of an integrated air cargo system infeasible in many areas. Thus, despite rapid economic growth, air carriers continue to provide relatively little air service between airports in Guangdong Province and the West.

Adding to China's dependence on Hong Kong's air cargo services is their need to incorporate foreign expertise into the distribution process. The business skills necessary for effective international trade include fluency in English, an understanding of modern business practices, familiarity with diverse cultural and legal environments, and proficiency in drafting complex contracts (Sung, 1991). Hong Kong's historical origins give local air cargo providers and freight forwarders a strong competitive advantage in providing these skill-intensive services. These advantages are likely to become even more important as Chinese exports become more differentiated, valuable, and complex.

The role of Hong Kong's air cargo industry is nowhere more important than in China's Special Economic Zones (SEZs), including Hainan, Shantou, Shenzhen, Xiamen, and Zhuhai. The low 15-percent corporate taxes, part of a tax structure authorized by the central government and modeled after Hong Kong's, are allowing the economies of the SEZs to grow at a rate almost twice that of China in general and six times that of the rest of the world. The amount of tonnage cargo shipped between the SEZs and Hong Kong's airport is rising by more than 20 percent per year (*Shippers Today*, 1992g) — a trend prompting investors to begin construction of a new Canton-Shantou toll road as well as to make improvements to the Kowloon-Canton railway. Finding the SEZs in need of improved transportation service, cargo airlines now coordinate their flight schedules with trucking firms and freight forwarders serving these regions. They are competing for the business of more than 4,500 foreign-invested enterprises, most with financial backing from Hong Kong, that have opened in the Pearl River Delta since 1986.

As the SEZs grow, shippers of air cargo have steadily migrated out of Hong Kong. This gives air cargo providers little choice but to redirect their marketing effort northward. China's SEZs offer such attractive conditions for manufacturing, including low wages and cheap land, that manufacturing activity within Hong Kong is declining. More than 80 percent of Hong Kong's factories have relocated labor- and land-intensive production to Guangdong Province over the past six years, greatly altering the region's character and landscape. The share of the Hong Kong gross domestic product attributable to manufacturing fell from 22 percent to 18 percent between 1987 and 1990 (*Shippers Today*, 1993d).

The rising prosperity of the SEZs not only is stimulating air cargo shipments from Hong Kong to Europe and North America, it is creating a new market for Hong Kong exports. In the last 14 years, per-capita income in South China has increased fourfold, stimulating discretionary spending. With more than 17,000 tonnes of air cargo moving north from Hong Kong to China annually, China is now the Hong Kong tenth largest air export destination. In the decade ahead, tonnage between Hong Kong and China is expected to continue to climb by more than 15 percent annually (*Shippers Today*, 1992c).

The opening of China gives the air cargo industry immense potential to grow. The Airport Authority in Hong Kong is forecasting 5 percent annual growth of air cargo tonnage through 2030. This is a conservative projection considering that air cargo shipments across Asian and transpacific routes are expected to continue growing by more than 9 percent annually — almost twice the Authority's forecast. (Air cargo tonnage is expected to grow by more than 6 percent annually even in North America and Europe, where a slower pace of economic growth is anticipated.) If such growth can be sustained, total cargo tonnage at Chek Lap Kok will rise 700 percent, to almost 6 million tonnes, by 2030 (Figure 1.3). Within 20 years, the number of freighter aircraft arriving and departing the airport will increase from the current level of about 12 per day to more than 60 per day. More than 95 percent of these planes are likely to be widebody Boeing 747s, which can handle more than 150,000 kilograms of cargo (*New Airport Master Plan*, 1992).

The continued growth of cargo services at Chek Lap Kok,

Figure 1.3. Air Cargo Growth Forecast

Annual Tonnage

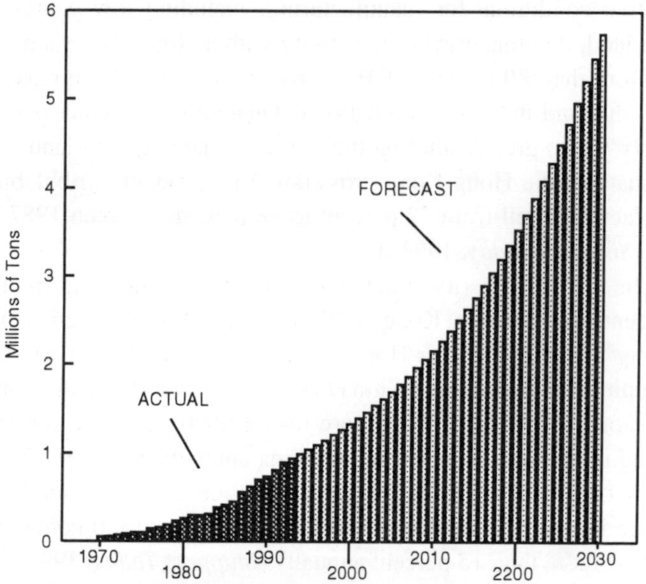

Sources: Provisional Airport Authority (1992) (Forecast).
Report on Civil Aviation, (1992) (Actual).

however, is by no means assured. Hong Kong is responding sluggishly to the challenges posed by growth-hungry airports throughout the region. Unless Hong Kong's policies are changed soon, services will be diverted to other parts of Asia. This will damage the financial condition of the new airport and undermine Hong Kong's ability to establish itself as a preeminent air cargo hub.

3. Competitive Threats

Throughout the Pacific Rim, countries are aggressively competing with Hong Kong for additional air cargo traffic:

- **Japan.** Japan is finishing its first round-the-clock airport, the Kansai International Airport near Osaka, which will provide an excellent regional alternative for trans-pacific freight originating in China. Although only half the size of Chek Lap Kok, it will open in late 1994 and will be able to capitalize on capacity shortages at Kai Tak. Major improvements to Tokyo's Narita Airport also are under way.

- **Macao.** The Macao territory is making plans to capitalize on Hong Kong's transitional period. Within five years of the 1995 opening of Macao's new international airport, officials hope to divert 4 million passengers away from Hong Kong — about 25 percent of Hong Kong's existing passenger market. Macao may encounter thorny bureaucratic problems in its bid to divert traffic from Hong Kong. (The territory reverts to Chinese sovereignty in 1999 and has not been given the right to negotiate its own air service agreements with foreign governments.) Nevertheless, Federal Express and other carriers have expressed interest in diverting some of their flights to Macao if Hong Kong user fees become excessive.
- **Malaysia.** Kuala Lumpur, already a major cargo center, is seeking to expand its share of the market by constructing a new airport 60 kilometers south of the existing one. The two-runway facility is expected to be completed by 1997.
- **Philippines.** Major improvements are planned for Manila's Ninoy Aquino Airport as well as the airport at Subic Bay, which is being vacated by the U.S. military. Both airports are vying to become major express cargo hubs.
- **South Korea.** South Korea is planning an airport near Seoul that will be larger than Chek Lap Kok and will be completed more quickly. South Korea's new diplomatic ties with Beijing should elevate the airport into a major transshipment center for Chinese products.
- **Singapore.** Changi Airport in Singapore, recently doubled in size, eventually will expand to four terminals and three runways — an expansion that Hong Kong will be unable to replicate.
- **Taiwan.** Officials in Taipei are drafting plans to make Chiang Kai Shek Airport the leading transportation center in Asia. Ultimately, the airport will have three runways and one of the world's largest cargo and passenger terminals.
- **Thailand.** The Thai Ministry of Transport recently approved a new airport, costing HK$23 billion, which is expected to be fully operational by 2002. Located 30 kilometers east of Bangkok, the new airport will have extensive cargo handling facilities.

- **China.** Finally, China is developing airport plans, calling for the construction or improvement of 22 new airports along the country's booming East Coast. Although these facilities could stimulate economic growth in all parts of China, they also render it urgent that Hong Kong adopt more market-oriented policies to assure the financial viability of its own airport project.

China is so eager to hasten the development of a modern air system that the Civil Aviation Administration of China (CAAC) recently announced an extraordinary new policy permitting its airlines to solicit foreign investment and managerial expertise (Westlake, 1992a). This new policy not only encourages foreign ownership of airline equity, but allows Chinese airlines to employ foreign nationals, hire consultants, and use outside expertise to upgrade existing airports or build new ones. Although few expect China to make major inroads into Hong Kong's air cargo market prior to 1997, the policy will help China siphon off much of the growth that Hong Kong would otherwise have enjoyed. The expected inflow of capital will accelerate the modernization of Chinese airlines and airports. Already, new nonstop cargo services linking Chinese cities with the United States and Europe are allowing many shippers to bypass Hong Kong's airport. Direct air shipments between China and the United States increased from 4,000 tonnes in 1980 to more than 70,000 tonnes in 1990 (McKee, 1991).

The most immediate Chinese alternative to Chek Lap Kok is less than 200 kilometers away. The Huangtian Airport in Shenzhen opened in October 1991 and will soon be China's second largest. This airport will complement the Baiyun International Airport in Guangzhou, where significant improvements also are under way. (China also has unveiled plans for a new airport in Guangzhou to be completed in 1997.) Shenzhen's proximity to the prospering Pearl River Delta and the New Territories has led 20 international airlines to begin negotiations for use of Huangtian Airport. One cargo carrier, Cargolux Airlines, already has made plans to begin service.

Shenzhen officials hope to capitalize on congestion at Kai Tak and the transition to Chek Lap Kok by offering low landing and cargo handling fees to attract the business of freight forwarders. By 1997, officials hope to handle half as much cargo as Hong Kong does (roughly 600,000 tonnes per year) and be able to finance a second runway. Shenzhen officials plan to improve convenience by allowing Hong Kong shippers to avoid Chinese customs and offering high-speed ferry service to Hong Kong, which will reduce travel time by about an hour. Shenzhen officials also will take advantage of the Chinese government's new policy allowing overseas freight forwarders and agents to work independently in the region — a move many consider to be an important logistical breakthrough.

These airport projects will lower shipping costs throughout South China. However, the entire region retains a tremendous stake in Hong Kong's air cargo industry. As the following chapter shows, Chek Lap Kok is the linchpin to improved air cargo services for all of South China.

Chapter 2

An Asian Hub for Express Cargo

The growth of the air cargo market is paving the way for the development of a major Asia–Pacific hub operation. Such a hub would, for the first time, allow express carriers to provide overnight delivery of cargo between hundreds of Asian commercial centers. Through coordinated, night-time flight connections, carriers would collect packages in the early evening and guarantee their delivery to another Asian destination the following morning. At least five cities — Hong Kong, Taipei, Manila, Shenzhen, and Singapore — are competing for the prize of a dominant air cargo hub. Hong Kong, however, has geographic and commercial advantages over the other sites.

1. The Expanding Express Market

Express cargo airlines fill a critical market niche. They provide faster service than traditional general operators through door-to-door delivery systems, comprehensive hub systems, and computerized tracking systems. Called "integrators" due to their vertically integrated air and ground services, they offer many ancillary services, including just-in-time delivery, guaranteed availability, and expedited customs clearance, to meet the needs of individual shippers. Although express cargo accounts for only 3 percent of total tonnage, it generates close to 20 percent of total air cargo revenues in Hong Kong.

Two types of express carriers serve Hong Kong: direct carriers, which operate their own aircraft; and indirect carriers, which do not operate aircraft but lease space on scheduled flights. Hong Kong is served by two U.S.-based direct carriers, Federal Express and United Parcel Service (UPS), which operate freighters *en route* to California;

and numerous indirect carriers, including DHL International, Ltd., a Hong Kong-based entity, TNT Express Worldwide, and Speedpost. Although DHL and TNT operate their own aircraft elsewhere, they have not yet joined the ranks of direct carriers in Hong Kong.

Federal Express, the largest of Hong Kong's express carriers, currently holds slightly more than one-third of the local express market, handling more than 150,000 packages each month. DHL and Speedpost each hold about 25 percent of the market, while UPS, TNT, and other firms hold the remaining 15 percent. Hong Kong-based airlines play a relatively small role in the express market. While Cathay Pacific operates a successful express business, Airport to Door Express (ADX), its customer base is relatively small and specialized.

The market for overnight document delivery in Hong Kong is growing by 30 percent annually (McKee, 1991). With its 14 local express delivery centers, DHL currently holds the largest share of this market. Despite computerization and the accessibility of facsimile machines, the volume of express shipments to the mainland is literally exploding, doubling each year, and is now 25 times larger than it was 20 years ago. Another rapidly expanding market segment is "global sourcing" services — logistics, distribution, and warehousing support for multinational companies needing fast delivery of inventory and replacement parts. Anticipating Asian growth, Federal Express recently established a global sourcing facility in Singapore as part of its Partsbank program. DHL is vigorously promoting a similar program called Interface in Singapore. The dynamism of these market segments is heightening the attractiveness of Hong Kong as a hub site.

Express carriers do not limit their business to small parcels, packages and other types of door-to-door traffic. As much as 85 percent of their cargo is airport-to-airport freight. At Federal Express, for example, daily flights are often filled with lower-priority cargo, much of it from customers predating the carrier's 1989 acquisition of Flying Tigers Airlines. Nevertheless, with emphasis on time-definite delivery, the carriers routinely charge higher prices for these shipments than general cargo carriers.

2. Asian Hub Opportunities

Shippers urgently need an Asian express hub. Although overnight express services are available currently in many Asian markets, the reliance on passenger aircraft to handle this cargo significantly reduces the quality of services provided. When passenger flights are used, shippers seeking overnight delivery often are required to deliver their packages as early as 9 a.m. on the preceding day, preventing the timely delivery of documents, spare parts, and other time-sensitive freight. Reliance on passenger flights also affects punctuality and can impede the development of electronic tracking systems which provide shippers with information about the status of their packages and parcels.

The North American market illustrates the untapped potential of an Asian express hub. Since launching the first hub-and-spoke system from Memphis, Tennessee, in 1973, Federal Express has enlarged its overnight operation to encompass more than 400 flights and 1.7 million packages daily. Customers can deliver their cargo to one of the airline's 1,400 customer service centres or 30,000 drop box locations, from which the cargo is delivered to the airport during the late evening hours (Federal Express, 1993). The carrier schedules its aircraft to depart from the outlying "spoke" destinations in the late evening and arrive nearly simultaneously at the hub between midnight and 1 a.m. Within two hours, cargo is quickly sorted in a specially designed terminal and reloaded onto planes bound for each shipment's final destination, where a fleet of 31,000 vehicles is available to deliver it to the customer's door. More than 99 percent of packages are delivered "on schedule," which requires comprehensive contingency plans and back-up systems at the hub.

Express services now generate more than 60 percent of the North American air cargo revenues. The number of domestic packages handled by North America's express carriers has more than doubled in recent years, rising from 350 million in 1986 to more than 800 million in 1993 (Dittler, 1992). The success of the Federal Express operation has prompted three other entities, UPS, DHL, and the U.S. Postal Services, to launch similar hub operations in Cincinnati, Ohio, Indianapolis, Illinois, Louisville, Kentucky, and Memphis, TN.

Computer systems play an integral role in the Federal Express operation. At the pick-up locations, the customer service agent uses a small, hand-held computer — a "Supertracker" — to record information about the shipment, including its destination and the type of service. The Supertracker instantly determines the best routing for the package. When the agent returns to his van or workstation, the data from the Supertracker is transmitted to the main computer network, "COSMOS." After COSMOS processes this information, it interacts with visual computer scanners to monitor the changing location and status of the package. Larger shippers can track the progress of their own shipments through on-site PowerShip terminals, which are directly linked to the COSMOS system (Federal Express, 1993).

Hub-and-spoke systems improve the efficiency of express services in several ways. By consolidating freight *en route* to many destinations onto a single plane, they enable airlines to use larger, more efficient aircraft. (The average price for an express shipment in the United States is less than US$15.) Large aircraft would be especially advantageous for an inter-Asia hub operator because of the long travel distances between cities. (The average flight distance for most North America hubs is less than 1,800 kilometers, compared with an expected average distance of 3,200 kilometers at an Asian hub.) The need for large aircraft to lower costs makes it unlikely that the Asian market can support more than one hub during the next decade. Hub-and-spoke systems also expand the range of services provided. They allow carriers to link a city to dozens of destinations with a single flight. A hub serving just 20 cities, for example, can provide overnight service to nearly 200 city pairs. Another advantage of hubbing is improved utilization of aircraft capacity through more predictable traffic flows. Pooling cargo bound for many destinations onto large planes lessens day-to-day fluctuations in demand, minimizing the amount of unused space per departure.

The world's four major express companies recognize the global potential of express cargo hubs. In Europe, for example, DHL, Federal Express, TNT, and UPS, are all expanding aggressively. DHL operates a hub in Brussels and is developing a same-day delivery system in Germany with Lufthansa Airlines; Federal Express is developing a hub operation in Paris; TNT is building a hub in Cologne, Germany; and UPS is developing an expensive ground-based delivery system throughout Western Europe.

These carriers are also preparing themselves for expanded inter-Asian services. Federal Express is experimenting with a small connecting complex in Taipei, from which it serves eight Asian destinations, including Hong Kong. Currently, this hub is used primarily to support that airline's trans-pacific operation and handles relatively little inter-Asia cargo. However, it is providing Federal Express with valuable Asian marketing experience for future expansion.[1] TNT recently launched a mini-hub in Manila to provide overnight service between four nations: Taiwan, Singapore, the Philippines, and Brunei. TNT, which currently uses two small planes, plans to enlarge this operation to 11 cities (Traffic World, 1993). DHL is demonstrating a strong interest in an Asian hub by investing in Singapore's Express Courier Center, proposing to finance and operate a major cargo terminal at Chek Lap Kok, and opening 14 new express centers on the mainland in 1993.

Although the impressive growth of inter-Asia market renders a hub inevitable, it will be a costly proposition. Airport curfews, bilateral treaties, seasonal fluctuations in demand, and a variety of logistical problems could hamper development. In addition, the incompatibility of flight schedules at the Asian hub and European and North American routes would require that the hub be essentially free standing. Nevertheless, key players in Hong Kong remain enthusiastic about a hub: the express airlines and Hong Kong's Provisional Airport Authority have commissioned major studies of the Asian express market.

The size of the future inter-Asia hub is less certain. By 2000, analysts project that it could generate as few as 10 additional

1. The carrier reportedly is considering opening an inter-Asian cargo hub in the Philippines, possibly at Subic Bay naval base in Manila. See Michael Di Cicco, "Federal Express to Establish Asian Hub at Former Naval Base, Philippines Says," *Journal of Commerce*, July 23, 1993.

departures daily (a relatively small hub serving only the largest airports) or as many as 25 additional departures daily (a medium-sized cargo hub serving all cities with major airports). Depending on its size, the hub could provide overnight service in 45 to 300 city pairs.

3. Hub Locational Issues

Hong Kong must act decisively to establish itself as a viable hub candidate. The hub's location will depend on at least five technical criteria: geography, local market, route authority, capacity, and service inputs.

(1) *Geography*. If all other factors were equal, the ideal hub location would be somewhere in the vicinity of Hong Kong, Manila, or Taipei — a location that would minimize total flight mileage and allow service with smaller, narrowbody aircraft (Figure 2.1). This makes airports in these three cities or Shenzhen very attractive as potential hubs. Singapore's Changi Airport, nearly 2,000 kilometers to the south, is a less attractive location.[2]

(2) *Local market*. A strong local market is another highly desirable characteristic, allowing carriers to generate much revenue at the hub itself. Singapore, Taiwan and Hong Kong, which handle more than 750,000 tonnes of cargo annually, have the most lucrative local markets. Manila and Shenzhen, currently handling only about 300,000 tonnes annually, are less attractive.

(3) *Route authority*. The legal authority to launch new flights within Asia is a prerequisite to a hub. Considering its restrictive aviation policies, Hong Kong currently is not a feasible hub site for

---

2. In many respects, Hong Kong's location is superior to the other prospective hub sites. I estimate that a Hong Kong hub could serve major Asian cargo centers with 6 percent fewer flight hours than a Taipei hub, 10 percent fewer flight hours than a Manila hub, and 36 percent fewer flight hours than a Singapore hub. This could reduce fuel expenses by HK$40 million annually. For a more thorough discussion, see my 1993 study, Express Air Cargo in the Pacific Rim: An Evaluation of Prospective Hub Sites, working paper, Public Service Program, DePaul University, Chicago, Illinois.

Figure 2.1. Potential Markets for Asian Express Hub

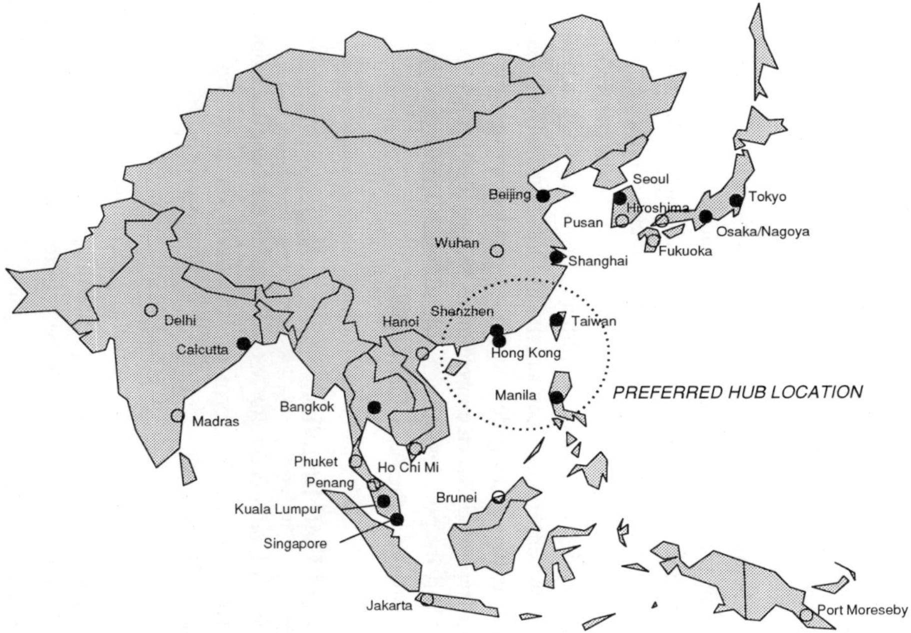

● PRIMARY DESTINATION. ANNUAL CARGO THROUGHPUT EXCEEDS 250,000 TONS.

○ SECONDARY DESTINATION. ANNUAL CARGO THROUGHPUT LESS THAN 250,000 TONS.

foreign carriers. Shenzhen, Taipei, Manila, and Singapore, with their more liberal aviation policies, are more accessible to foreign carriers.

(4) *Capacity*. Adequate airport capacity is critical. This eventually will be available at all five sites, but Hong Kong will be unable to accommodate a hub until the opening of Chek Lap Kok in 1997 — a notable disadvantage. The other airports will be able to accommodate a hub as early as 1995.

(5) *Service inputs*. Finally, the hub must offer ancillary services, including high-quality maintenance services, terminal services, and labor. Of these, terminal facilities are likely to be the most decisive. Singapore, Shenzhen, and Manila, with their commitment to modern, competitive terminal facilities, have decisive advantages over Hong Kong, which has not yet committed to providing such facilities.

At present, no city can satisfy all five criteria. Hong Kong must overcome two glaring deficiencies — inadequate terminal facilities and restrictive air service agreements before it becomes a viable hub site. Until its policies change, Manila and Taipei may become the frontrunners for the Asia–Pacific hub.

4. Local Hub Benefits

The South China economy would reap direct benefits from a Chek Lap Kok hub in the form of improved services and increased aeronautical revenues.

- Improved Services. A Hong Kong express hub would provide more attractive "close out" times (i.e., terminal deadlines) and offer more nonstop service to the regional shippers than would an offshore hub. Regional shippers would be able to deliver cargo to Chek Lap Kok as late as 10 p.m. for overnight shipment if that airport were to become a hub. (The deadline would be about 5 p.m. if Chek Lap Kok were merely a "spoke" for an offshore hub.) This would be particularly beneficial to South China's SEZ, including Shantou, Hainan, and Xiamen, which remain too small to support their own flights to an offshore hub. They will continue to depend on Hong Kong (or Shenzhen) for air service. A local hub also would lead to lower terminal rates and hasten the development of an advanced electronic data interchange (EDI) system in South China.

The most important benefit of a local hub would be enhanced competition. Based on analysis to be presented in Chapter 4, increased competition from a hub operator would lower the price of cargo shipments from Hong Kong by as much as 5 percent. Even considering the local airlines' revenue losses due to this price reduction, estimated at between HK$146 million and HK$244 million, a hub would provide substantial net benefits to the South China economy, ranging from HK$278 million (based on a 3-percent price reduction scenario) to HK$464 million annually (based on a 5-percent price reduction scenario).

- Aeronautical Revenues. A local hub would provide substantial new revenues for the Airport Authority in Hong Kong through increased landing and parking fee receipts. Although Hong Kong plans to observe the rules of the International Air Transport Association, which prohibits airports from charging airport user fees in excess of long-run average costs, fees at Chek Lap Kok nevertheless will be much higher than short-run marginal costs. Much of the revenue generated could be used toward the timely retirement of the airport's debt.

A few calculations illustrate the vast revenue potential of a hub. If an even mix of widebody and narrowbody aircraft served the hub, each departure would generate about HK$32,700 in parking and landing fees daily[3]. Assuming that the hub operates six days per week, the annual increase in *gross* revenue would range between HK$102 million and HK$255 million. Most of these revenues would directly improve the airport authority's financial position. The PAA expects to apply as much as 70 percent of the aeronautical revenues generated during the new airport's first five years of operation toward the retirement of debt (*New Airport Master Plan*, 1992). However, if it is assumed, as a worst-case scenario, that only half of the additional user

3. These user fee projections are based on estimates published in Provisional Airport Authority statements. Actual aeronautical revenues will depend on the amount and distribution of cargo on departing flights.

fee receipts would be available for debt repayment (the other half would cover incremental expenses, such as air traffic control costs and ancillary airport services), the annual net benefits from these revenues would be between HK$51 million and HK$127 million, depending on the size of the hub.

These three scenarios suggest that the direct benefits of an express cargo hub to shippers and consumers of Hong Kong would range from HK$329 million to HK$591 million per year (Table 2.1). The most likely outcome, Scenario B, suggests an annual gain of HK$448 million. In terms of net present value (using a 6-percent discount rate), the hub would directly benefit the region by HK$2.4 billion to HK$4.4 billion in its first decade of operation.

These are lower-bound estimates. They ignore the benefits of increased activity on commercial revenues, franchise fees, and land rentals around the airport. They also ignore the benefits enjoyed by shippers and the local economy due to better service and investments in infrastructure by air carriers. Indirect benefits may include additional profits for ground handlers, freight forwarders, terminal operators, and airlines. Of course, airports in South China may experience some revenue losses due to Chek Lap Kok's development as a hub, but these losses are likely to be small.

A cargo hub would also give the Airport Authority other

Table 2.1. Express Cargo Hub Benefit Assessment

	Scenario A	Scenario B	Scenario C
Incremental Flight Activity			
Average price reduction	3%	4%	5%
Daily flight departures	10	15	25
Incremental Benefits (millions)			
Shipper benefits	HK$278	HK$371	HK$464
Aeronautical revenues*	HK$ 51	HK$ 77	HK$127
Net Annual Benefits (millions)	HK$329	HK$448	HK$591
Present Value (billions)***	HK$ 2.4	HK$ 3.3	HK$ 4.4

* Net contribution after costs.

** Based on a 3-percent fee.

*** Assumes 6-percent discount and 10-year time horizon.

opportunities to generate revenue for debt servicing. Airports throughout the world are turning toward new types of user fees, ranging from fuel surcharges to tonnage taxes, and terminal facility charges, to offset high construction costs. One possible source of revenue for Hong Kong would be a value-added fee on express cargo. The simplest type of fee would be based on the total value of the "airbill," which is the invoice showing the amount of money the shipper is paying to transport the freight.

Additional research will be needed to determine whether value-added fees would threaten the attractiveness of Hong Kong as a hub site. However, considering the advantages of Hong Kong's location, a small fee that would be eliminated as soon as the airport's debt is fully retired could have minimal impact on business. While no major airport has implemented a value-added fee (several have proposed them), Hong Kong would have the opportunity to use this tool to help defray some of the airport's HK$171 billion cost.

The revenue potential of a 3-percent value-added fee is impressive. Conservatively estimated, an express cargo hub in Hong Kong would divert 3 percent to 7.5 percent of inter-Asia cargo traffic through Chek Lap Kok. (This estimate is based on the share of traffic moving through the hubs of express cargo carriers in trans-Pacific markets and suggests an annual volume ranging from 156,000 to 390,000 tonnes.) Because the airbill value would be about HK$30,000 per ton, or about HK$30 per kilogram, the fee would generate between HK$140 million and HK$351 million annually. These additional proceeds would allow debt servicing to be accelerated by 3.5 percent to 8.8 percent.

5. Political Uncertainty and Hub Development

For a hub at Chek Lap Kok to become a reality, Hong Kong must not only improve terminal services and adopt less restrictive aviation policies, it must cope with the vagaries of international diplomacy.

Restoration of Sovereignty

Uncertainties about restoration of sovereignty over Hong Kong to China in 1997 loom large in the minds of some potential hub operators. For brevity's sake, let us consider only the most essential aspects of the restoration of sovereignty for the air cargo industry. These facts illustrate that an air cargo hub remains a viable proposition for Hong Kong, despite apprehension about unresolved political issues.

Although negotiations between Hong Kong and Beijing remain awkward and tense, China appears prepared to grant the full range of economic freedoms specified in the Sino-British Joint Declaration, which specifies that the rights and lifestyles currently enjoyed by Hong Kong residents are to be preserved for a 50-year period after 1997. Hong Kong will become a Special Administrative Region (SAR) with substantial authority for self-governance.

In a Memorandum of Understanding, signed with the government of Great Britain, China gave its "firm support" to the new airport. However, air cargo providers acknowledge that China's real support of the project remains lukewarm, especially pertaining to debt financing, which will account for about two-thirds of the project's HK$171 billion cost. China has serious concerns about the long-range implications of this debt for the future SAR government (Westlake, 1992). If China continues to question the project's financing plan, the enthusiasm potential hub operators could wane.

The financial issues are too complex for full renumeration here. Among Beijing's biggest objections is Hong Kong's planned use of the SAR Land Fund proceeds to pay for the new airport. Beijing believes the SAR Land Fund — consisting of half the proceeds from the governmental sale of real estate — should be earmarked for use by the Hong Kong SAR government after 1997. According to the Joint Declaration, the SAR Land Fund can be spent only with Beijing's approval. However, Hong Kong officials maintain the Joint Declaration authorizes them to use the proceeds for basic infrastructure and public works projects, including airport projects. Local officials note that the fund's HK$25 billion balance will continue to grow through 1997, leaving an ample amount of money for the new government (Westlake, 1992). Some financial officials believe that the actual balance of the fund will be as high as HK$75 billion by 1997, an amount greater than that which the Joint Declaration requires.

Another uncertainty is the future labor market. The much publicized "brain drain" has been a difficult personnel issue for airlines and ground service providers, especially the Hong Kong Aircraft Engineering Company (HAECO), which lost more than 20 percent of its skilled employees between 1989 and 1991. Many transportation planners working in Hong Kong's civil service corps joined ranks with the estimated 1,200 people per week who emigrated from Hong Kong during 1990 and 1991 (*Hong Kong Standard*, 1989). Cargo airlines and terminal operators are concerned that skilled aviation employees will make use of their so-called "insurance policy" — foreign passports that permit them to leave if the political and economic situation deteriorates after 1997.

These concerns are not to be trivialized. However, the highly publicized debate thus far has had little effect on the expansion plans of carriers. Most believe that the airport will be completed close to schedule and will serve as an ideal hub site.

Changing Asian Diplomacy

The strained bilateral negotiation process between the United States and China is a more immediate concern to potential hub operators. Over the past few years, these nations have focused their attention on the Section 301 Trade Act, enacted by the United States in response to China's infringement of individual rights after the Tiananman Square crisis. As part of this dispute, the United States threatened to invoke US$1.5 billion in retaliatory tariffs against China — a move that would have had disastrous effects on air cargo carriers, suppressing air traffic by as much as 40 percent. Protectionist sentiment in the United States is being fueled by China's US$12 billion trade surplus and the election of a president who is less amenable to free trade than was his predecessor. Air cargo providers, understandably relieved when the United States and China tentatively resolved their trade dispute in late 1992, remain wary about the future of this damaged trade relationship.

Potential hub operators are also apprehensive about the North American Free Trade Agreement (NAFTA), which will be considered for ratification soon. This agreement strips away trade tariffs between Mexico, Canada and the United States. With its skilled labor force and low wages, Mexico may become a competitor of Hong Kong. Some shippers fear that NAFTA will become an implicit extension of the Monroe Doctrine, a policy promoting the idea that life on the American continent should be free from foreign influence. Others fear that NAFTA will lead to systematic bureaucratic favoritism for products of North American origin.

Finally, Hong Kong's attractiveness as a hub site could diminish if South Korea and Taiwan, which account for nearly 20 percent of all airborne trade, can agree to more liberal trade arrangements with China. In the not-too-distant future, Seoul and Taipei will be promoting their improved infrastructures as viable alternatives to Hong Kong for Asian and North American freight.

The vagaries of international diplomacy will undoubtedly play a role in Chek Lap Kok's future. However, the outlook is favorable. The five proposals submitted to operate terminals at Chek Lap Kok show that air cargo providers consider Hong Kong to be a sound investment.

Chapter 3

A Proposal for Competitive Terminals

Terminal services must become more differentiated and made more accommodating to airlines' changing needs if Chek Lap Kok is to reach its potential as a major cargo hub. The proposal outlined below calls for four steps to be taken by the Provisional Airport Authority:

- Award licenses to two independent terminal operators (or three operators if additional space can be made available for cargo terminals) with each operator authorized to handle both express and general cargo.
- Choose one company affiliated with an express carrier to operate a terminal that offers a separate, dedicated area for express cargo.
- Give terminal operators complete freedom in pricing, encouraging competition to eliminate the need for regulation of prices or profits.
- Charge each terminal operator a flat license fee proportional to its use of airport land. Choose terminal operators on the basis of the strength of their proposals, thus avoiding an "open tender" bidding system.

Background information about the Chek Lap Kok project and answers to questions about the details of the proposal illuminate its benefits to the South China economy.

1. What Is the Status of the Chek Lap Kok Project?

The new airport is part of the Airport Core Programme, which it is estimated will cost HK$171 billion, inclusive of the ancillary road and rail links. The Airport Core Programme is part of the Port and Airport Development Strategy (PADS), which includes new container ports at Stonecutters and Tsing Yi islands (HK$50 billion), a new "cargo village" adjacent to the airport at Tung Chung (HK$38 million), and extensive highway and infrastructure facilities (Figure 3.1) (Tong, 1991).[1] However, the Hong Kong government is making the airport the top priority of PADS; it is demonstrating this commitment by scheduling its opening in 1997, the same year Hong Kong reverts to Chinese sovereignty.

To make room for the airport, Chek Lap Kok, an uninhabited island off the coast of Lantau, and Lam Chau, a smaller island, are being leveled and 940 hectares of seabed are being reclaimed. After reducing these islands to a height of six meters, engineers will have created a new island of 1,248 hectares, a site five times the size of the existing airport at Kai Tak. By 1997, a single runway, an expansive terminal complex, and support facilities will be complete. The second runway will be built as demand dictates, bringing total capacity to 87 million passengers and 10 million pounds of cargo — approximately a 500 percent greater capacity than that of Kai Tak Airport.

Chek Lap Kok will be run primarily by commercial entities, much like the Mass Transit Railway Corporation (MTRC) of Hong Kong. The most important of these entities is the Provisional Airport Authority (PAA), which is designing, managing, and promoting the new airport. (The PAA will be renamed the Airport Authority after the

1. Considering the government's track record on major projects, the cost of the airport is likely to exceed initial projections by 25 percent or more (Tong, 1991). Air cargo providers have a particular interest in the Lantau Fixed Crossing, an expensive highway project connecting the airport with Kowloon. The Crossing will include the world's longest suspension bridge, spanning 1,400 meters, which must accommodate virtually all cargo transported to and from Check Lap Kok. (No cargo is expected to be transported over the rail links.)

Figure 3.1. Port and Airport Development Strategy

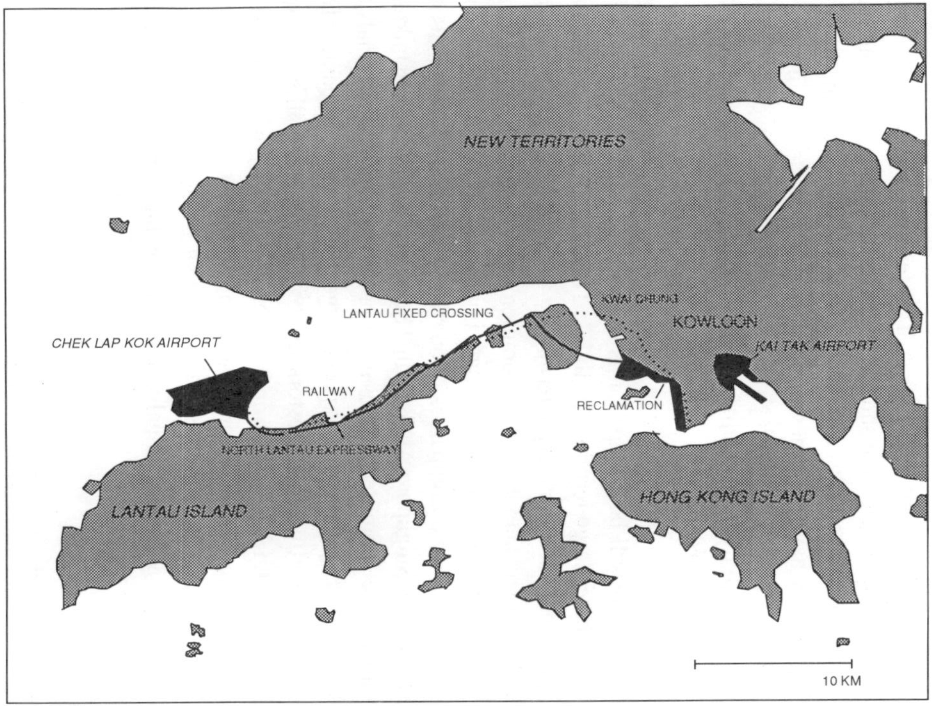

project's completion.) The PAA hopes to retire all debt by 2005 — an extraordinarily fast payback period — and must enjoy rapid and uninterrupted growth of air cargo services to achieve this goal.[2]

Cargo terminals will occupy a rectangular quadrant at Chek Lap Kok's southern end (Figure 3.2). This terminal complex, the world's largest, will employ the same type of vertical design and automation system that is being used at Kai Tak, but will be more than three times longer and have 12 times the capacity. The close proximity of the terminals to the cargo village at Tung Chung, only a five-minute drive via an auxiliary bridge, will provide convenient access to shippers and freight forwarders.

Twenty-two hectares are set aside for these terminals. Although conditions will be cramped, this site can accommodate two (or possibly three) large terminal facilities. The PAA is reluctant to allocate additional land for cargo terminals because this would require a reduction in land for other commercial activities. Five companies have submitted proposals to plan, build, and operate cargo terminals on the site. Two companies, Hong Kong Air Cargo Terminals Ltd. (HACTL), Singapore Air Terminal Services (SATS), and an unknown entity have submitted proposals to provide integrated terminals that handle both general and express cargo. Two other companies, DHL and a consortium of investors led by Changi International Airport Services (CIAS), including Federal Express, have submitted proposals for express cargo terminals. The PAA is officially undecided about the number of licenses that it award and is scheduled to finalize airport terminal decisions not later than the middle of 1994.

2. The user fees paid to the Airport Authority by cargo airlines will be much higher at the new airport than at Kai Tak. Aeronautical charges, for example, will be increased by more than 300 percent between 1993 and 1997. (Cargo airlines currently pay an average of HK$10,000 per flight in landing and parking fees.) Although the Hong Kong government currently is the sole shareholder of the Authority, full or partial privatization remains a distinct possibility.

Figure 3.2. Master Plan—Chek Lap Kok

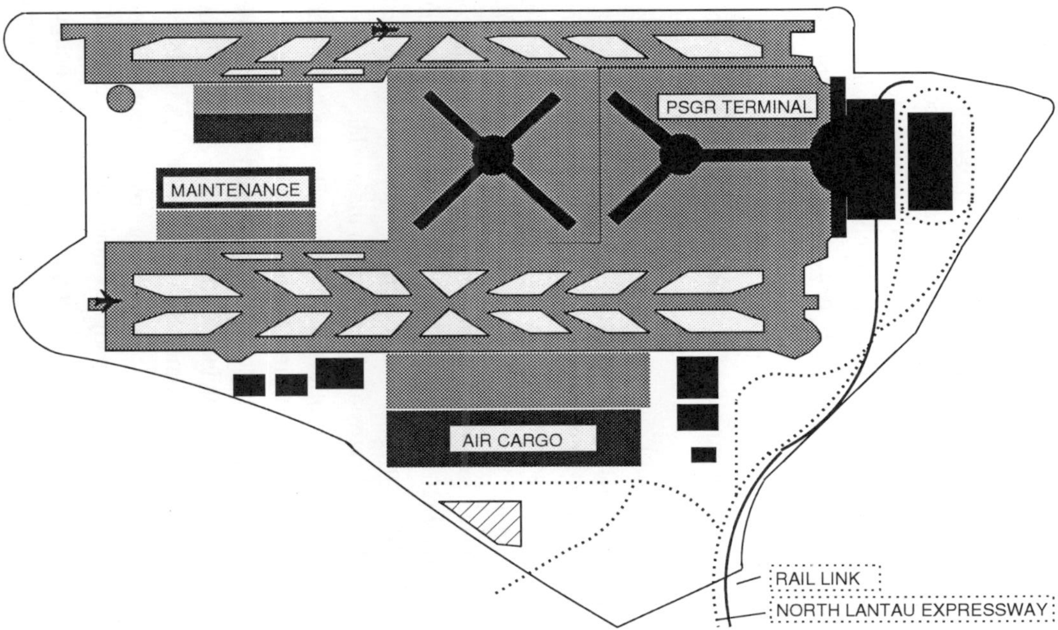

2. How Are Cargo Terminals in Hong Kong Currently Managed and Operated?

Under an exclusive license with the Hong Kong government, HACTL currently owns and operates all cargo terminal facilities at Kai Tak Airport. All of Hong Kong's airborne freight moves through one of HACTL's two terminals, where it is either placed in storage, transferred to other airlines, or picked up by freight forwarders, trucking companies or shippers. (The company's subsidiary, Hong Kong Cargo Industry Services, is called upon to perform some of these tasks.) Governmental regulations limit HACTL's profits to 12.5 percent of its assets.

This arrangement makes Kai Tak the world's largest cargo airport served by only a single terminal operator. HACTL's exclusive license was awarded in 1976 in response to shortages of land at the airport — a problem that prevents express carriers from independently operating terminals, an arrangement that they strongly prefer, and requires HACTL to use advanced technology to meet the growing demand. For example, Terminal 2, the larger of Kai Tak's two facilities which was opened in 1991, has automatic stacker cranes that can quickly locate and retrieve any of 2,240 storage containers inside. At seven stories high and with full computerization, it is the largest and most technologically advanced terminal in the world.

HACTL is an influential player in Hong Kong aviation policy. Swire Pacific and Jardine Matheson, another major conglomerate, each hold a 30-percent stake in the company. (Swire's other aviation-related subsidiaries include Cathay Pacific Airlines, Dragonair, and Hong Kong Air Terminal Services.) HACTL's influence was enhanced recently when the Hong Kong government relinquished its 10 percent stake in the company to China National Aviation Corporation (CNAC), the same holding company that recently bought a stake in Cathay Pacific. CNAC's presence adds an important diplomatic dimension to the upcoming licensing decisions at Chek Lap Kok, giving this Chinese entity a financial stake in the terminal operator's future.

3. Why Is Competition among Terminal Operators Essential to Chek Lap Kok's Future as a Hub?

Terminal services are often the only link in the lengthy, worldwide distribution chain where carriers cannot exercise complete control over service quality. This renders the link susceptible to communication breakdowns, disputes, and delays. Carriers understand that the quality of terminal services can be guaranteed only by operating their own terminals (an infeasible option at Chek Lap Kok) or negotiating and bargaining directly with terminal operators in an unfettered, competitive marketplace.

The Need for Competition

The South China region will not stay at the forefront of Asia's air cargo industry without a market-oriented terminal approach. The spectacular growth in volume and services will require risk-taking and innovation at all levels of the cargo distribution chain. The existing system, which authorizes a regulated monopoly to provide all terminal services, is not sufficiently versatile or responsive to effectively serve the region. By virtually guaranteeing profits and giving local customers few alternatives, it dampens the incentive for terminal operators to aggressively introduce new products or respond swiftly to carriers' requests for special services. It should be noted that none of the 10 largest express hubs worldwide uses the services of a monopoly terminal provider.

HACTL's services exemplify some of these problems. Although many shippers have been served well by HACTL (it mishandled less than 0.1 percent of its consignments in 1991, compared to a mishandling rate of more than 2 percent at other major Asian airports), the company has developed a reputation as an unenthusiastic player in the express cargo market. It demonstrates this lack of enthusiasm through its risk aversion and its frequent rejections of carriers' requests for new services. (HACTL has dismissed some of these requests as mere attempts to "get an edge" on competitors, not acknowledging that such services offer real benefits for consumers (*Executive*, 1992).)

Regulatory protection may also explain why HACTL initially was skeptical about the need for a separate area for express cargo at the new airport — a skepticism shared by few other industry participants.

The proposal calls for the PAA to foster competition by awarding licenses to at least two terminal operators (or three if additional land can be made available) and to permit each operator to handle both express and general cargo. At least one terminal would be designed and operated by express airlines.

A competitive approach would enhance service quality in at least four ways:

(1) *Opportunities for Manual Intervention and Quality Control.* The suggested approach would encourage terminal operators to give carriers the authority they need to manually intervene in the terminal process, facilitating quality control. Terminal operators would have the impetus to lease terminal space and allow carriers to use their own terminal handling equipment, develop their own on-site operating procedures, and provide their own freight warehouse in local terminals — services that have not been provided under the existing monopoly system. This would enable carriers to expedite late shipments and use portable scanners within the terminal to update their data bases.

Direct intervention and specialized terminal services are an integral part of all major express hubs, including the Federal Express "Superhub" in Memphis, TN. At this hub, packages are unloaded from planes onto an elevator and placed on a conveyor belt, where airline employees assign a destination code (i.e., the zip code) to each package. The packages travel along the quarter-mile conveyor to the "Primary Matrix," where 84 automated conveyor belts automatically sort the cargo according to its destination. The zip code printed on each package alerts an electric eye, which activates an electric arm to push packages onto another conveyor belt. At this point, employees conduct a manual, secondary sort, and load packages onto a container for shipment to the destination. Finally, before loading this cargo onto another plane, another group of employees scan the packages with a hand-held "Supertracker" to make sure that it is in the right place. With an elapsed time of only two hours and 15 minutes between the last plane's arrival and the last plane's departure, this highly specialized process must be completed flawlessly.

Terminals operated by regulated monopolists seldom permit carriers to engage in such extensive intervention, denying them access to "critical sort points," or locations where shipments are classified and prioritized. HACTL's proposal to be the sole operator at Chek Lap Kok attempts to address these problems by providing carriers with segregated customs facilities, direct access to the airport apron, and separate areas within the terminal for secondary cargo sorting. These are all valuable innovations. However, its proposal remains unsatisfactory because it does not provide express carriers with direct access to several critical sort points, thus creating a so-called "black hole" in the quality control process (*Executive*, 1992). Nor can HACTL's proposal to be the only terminal provider overcome the inherent limitations of any monopoly arrangement, which reduces a terminal operator's incentive to respond quickly to changing industry needs.

(2) *Contingency Planning*. The suggested approach would greatly enhance opportunities for contingency planning. It would encourage terminal operators to allow airlines to alter their procedures in the event of inclement weather, mechanical problems, or schedule irregularities. When emergencies occur, carriers would be able to sort and prioritize their shipments quickly. Such routine occurrences cannot be handled effectively through negotiations with regulated terminal providers.

Monopoly providers tend to be unsympathetic to the need for contingency planning. Without a large stake in the financial success of express airlines, they typically establish inflexible deadlines for the loading and unloading of aircraft cargo. Their rigid deadlines often require carriers' vans to make two rounds of deliveries instead of one, thus doubling fuel and labor costs, and leading to missed connections and poor aircraft utilization. Terminals operating under competitive conditions have little choice but to adopt more fluid deadlines.

(3) *Product Differentiation*. The suggested approach would give carriers the opportunities they need to expand and diversify their service offerings. Express carriers are warehousing experts, logistics specialists, and transportation providers. To keep pace with their

competitors, they must continually introduce new products or innovations. A single operator, facing strong pressure to provide a uniform product to all customers, would be less than willing to respond to the need for new and non-conventional services. Examples of recently introduced services include UPS's Expedited Package Service, which provides low-cost, guaranteed delivery anywhere in the world within four days; Federal Express' Powership 2 Service, which provides instant tracking information for frequent shippers; and DHL's expanding network of Just-in-Time warehousing services.

(4) *Insulation from Political Uncertainty*. Finally, competition would help insulate carriers from many of the political uncertainties associated with the restoration of sovereignty over Hong Kong to China, reducing their apprehension about the quality of airport services after 1997. This would help stabilize their investments. (Although Chek Lap Kok Airport will be beyond Chinese control, the CNAC's equity stake in HACTL could make this partisan player an active voice in terminal planning.) Competitive arrangements also would alleviate potential conflicts of interest associated with monopoly providers. Express airlines, for example, pose a formidable threat to airlines that have an equity stake in HACTL, which could put the operator in an awkward position with its influential airline stockholders. Although HACTL has been even-handed in the past, the expansion of express carriers into inter-Asian markets could escalate favoritism concerns if that company were to retain its monopoly.

Opportunities for Vertical Integration

The proposal calls for one terminal to be directly owned and operated by express airlines. This would further enhance opportunities for quality control and product differentiation. Such "vertical integration" would let carriers become more actively involved in terminal design and management, thus enabling them to respond more quickly to shippers' needs and avoid costly negotiations with third-party terminal operators. Rather than emphasizing *economies of scale*, carriers may choose to develop a terminal that emphasizes *economies of scope,* keeping costs low by allowing companies to allocate their overhead across many different product lines.

The advantages of vertical integration in terminal services can be best understood against the backdrop of the broader global trend toward more flexible production processes. Japanese businesses, for example, have redesigned large segments of their economies to emphasize economies of scope rather than economies of scale. The country's automobile assembly plants have been rebuilt to allow maximum versatility, allowing rapid adjustments to products in response to changing consumer tastes (*Fortune*, 1992).

The widespread versatility that can be achieved at air cargo terminals is exemplified at the Express Courier Centre in Singapore's Changi Airport. This facility, which opened in October 1992, is operated by Singapore Airport Terminal Services (SATS). It provides leased office and warehouse space to major express carriers and has proven so successful that SATS is planning to build a similar, larger facility before the end of the decade. The *recovery time* (the time required to process and inspect cargo) at this new facility averages 25 to 30 minutes — one-fourth the recovery time at Kai Tak's terminals. DHL International has made the largest investment in the facility, and has more than 23,000 square meters of floor space. Finding it an excellent prototype for Hong Kong, DHL is using the Centre as the basis for its proposed terminal at Chek Lap Kok (DHL, 1993).

To assure that carriers in Hong Kong are provided with the same speed and flexibility as those in Singapore, the proposal calls for at least one terminal to offer a separate, dedicated area for express cargo. Reliability and speed suffer when high-priority cargo share the same facility with low-priority cargo. Congestion can delay urgent shipments. This problem is evident at Kai Tak. Recovery time is three to four hours for express cargo and the *minimum connect time* (the time required for cargo to make transfers between flights) is at least three hours — a situation untenable for carriers seeking to operate an express hub.

A separate area for express cargo will be costly. Carriers will need to separate express and general cargo when unloading their planes. These dual facilities will also require the government to oversee separate customs offices. But the worldwide movement toward state-of-the-art cargo facilities shows that the benefits of separate facilities for express carpriers more than offset these costs. While officials in Hong Kong remain noncommittal, those in Manila, Seoul, Shenzhen, and Taipei are offering, or planning to offer, dedicated express cargo areas. Most major participants, including the airlines, HACTL and the Hong Kong Shippers Council, agree that separate express and general cargo facilities should be included in the Chek Lap Kok design.

Opposition to Competition

Not everyone agrees that competitive terminals are best for the region. The Hong Kong Association of Freight Forwarding Agents, the Hong Kong Shippers Council, and the Hong Kong Coalition of Service Industries, for example, have gone on record as supporting a continuation of the existing regulated monopoly scheme. HACTL has also been vocal in expressing its view that ending its tenure as the sole proprietor of terminal services would be unwise and unfair — a "retrograde step." (The retention of an exclusive license is considered so important to HACTL and its 1,800 employees that an extensive lobbying campaign is underway.) The terminal operator has even hinted that it may be uninterested in an operation at Chek Lap Kok if it is not awarded a monopoly license.

Supporters of the single-operator arrangement contend that a monopoly would enhance the efficiency of terminal operations by facilitating economies of scale. They maintain that a single operator would simplify aircraft operations and allow carriers to share storage space and loading and unloading areas. A problem with this economies-of-scale justification is that it reduces terminal services to a featureless commodity with no regard for product differentiation. This view is inconsistent with the experience of virtually every major airport in Europe and North America, where specialization and niche-filling have become integral parts of competitive terminal markets. Express carriers strongly prefer smaller and more versatile terminal operators, despite their higher costs.

Others argue that a single operator is necessary because it would be more convenient for freight forwarders and other ground handlers, allowing them to interact with one entity. This position underestimates the adaptability of these institutions. It assumes that freight forwarders are static, low-technology enterprises unable to respond to new market conditions. This view is unrealistic: forwarders in Hong Kong are dynamic and resilient in the face of change. The threat of market share loss to integrated carriers such as Federal Express and UPS is encouraging forwarders to rapidly improve both their services and their marketing approaches. Many forwarders are providing, for the first time, door-to-door and global sourcing services. (Their research shows that by the end of the decade, more than 90 percent of cargo will move from door to door, compared with 50 percent in 1992.) Forwarders are providing more "guaranteed uplift" services, or assurances to customers that their freight will depart on a certain day. They are beginning to offer shippers financial services that traditionally have been available only through banks. These types of innovations would not have occurred had policymakers protected forwarders on the basis of their purported inability to change.

To protect market share, forwarders are also improving their computerized tracking systems so that they can provide instant information about a shipment's status. These services have been improving steadily since 1991, when Hong Kong's forwarders gained access to an Electronic Data Interchange (EDI) communications network. This was made possible through an agreement between Hong Kong Telecom and Global Logistics System Asia. EDI provides worldwide access to air cargo information, paving the way to a "paperless" trading system (*Shippers Today*, 1992f). It will also enhance their ability to work simultaneously with several terminal operators.

Perhaps most importantly, the evolving marketplace is encouraging smaller forwarding companies to consolidate with large, international forwarding networks. This is improving their marketing effectiveness, their ability to bargain with airlines for favorable rates, and their ground delivery systems. The advantages of consolidation will grow as airlines move to acquire ground delivery systems, as Lufthansa and Japan Airlines recently did by acquiring a 51 percent stake in DHL International, Ltd. Some analysts expect consolidation to accelerate after the opening of Chek Lap Kok, which will increase the distance between forwarders and their customers by more than 30 kilometers. Shippers would have been denied these improvements had policymakers acted on the requests of forwarders to protect the *status quo*.

A final objection to a multi-terminal system is that most cargo probably would be shipped through a HACTL-operated terminal even if competitive terminals were available at Chek Lap Kok. HACTL's biggest stockholders are the parent companies of Cathay Pacific, Dragonair, and various Chinese airlines. As a result, HACTL is virtually guaranteed a 50 percent share of the terminal business if it is awarded a license. However, this would not thwart competition. The opportunity for large foreign carriers to switch terminals would give them considerable leverage in negotiations. Because marginal costs are only a small fraction of the total costs associated with terminals (many costs are fixed in the form of overhead expense), a small dip in market share would translate into a significant loss in profits.

4. Why Should Terminal Rates Be Unregulated?

Competition between terminal operators would keep prices at attractive levels, hasten the development of more sophisticated pricing systems, and encourage the efficient use of cargo terminals. As terminal operators move away from the existing one-price-fits-all rate structure, they would develop rates that reflect the marginal costs of providing various cargo services. For example, cargo that is late to arrive, difficult to handle, or costly to store would be handled at a higher rate, thus sending appropriate market signals to shippers and airlines. These innovations would supplement the efforts of airport authorities to develop comprehensive pricing systems that encourage flights during off-peak periods and discourage highway traffic around the airport during peak periods.

A two-operator ("duopoly") system, of course, may not provide the same level of price competition as a multi-terminal system. However, several local organizations are mistaken in their conclusion that a cartel would inevitably form which would mitigate any of the purported benefits of competition. (The apparent formation of a cartel at Kwai Chung container terminals frequently is cited in support of a monopoly arrangement.) Although concern about a cartel is not entirely unfounded, the formation of a stable cartel is far less likely than most have been led to believe.

Cartels tend to be unstable when members have opportunities to expand their output at the expense of other cartel members. At Kwai Chung, cartel members have little opportunity to do this due to chronic shortage of capacity. Members are not inclined to "chisel" on a cartel because it is virtually impossible for them to accommodate additional business. This would not be the case at Chek Lap Kok, where there would be ample room for additional business, giving cartel members strong incentives to secretly undercut the agreed-upon price or output level. In addition, carriers might attempt to circumvent the cartel's price by luring business from other cartel members through superior service.

Also lessening the stability of a cartel would be the rising price elasticity of demand (i.e., price sensitivity) for cargo terminal services. Terminal rates held high by a cartel would suppress volume. With the opening of regional airports, including those in Shenzhen, Macau, and Guangzhou, airlines will have viable alternatives to Chek Lap Kok and will use these alternatives to gain leverage in negotiations with local terminal operators.

Authorizing express carriers to operate at least one terminal would similarly lessen cartel risk. Express carriers are "newcomers" to the Hong Kong aviation scene and can be expected to manage their terminals differently than locally owned terminals. Their presence would render the terms of a cartel difficult to enforce. Moreover, as express carriers would be both suppliers and demanders of terminal services, they would be less enthusiastic about cartel pricing if they had to directly bear some of the consequences of their terminal subsidiary's pricing practices.

The airport authority could, as a last resort, re-establish regulations to keep prices at competitive levels if a stable cartel were to develop. A "scheme of control" governing terminal operators could be reinstituted swiftly. The least damaging approach would be a series of price ceilings (i.e., maximum prices), which would permit price competition and still be relatively easy for the airport authority to enforce. A more cumbersome method would be an extension of the existing scheme of control, which limits the profits of terminal operators to a designated percentage of gross assets. However, the regulatory path would be a poor substitute for competition under any type of terminal arrangement. While it has the potential to keep prices low, regulation dampens incentives for innovation and efficiency. Price regulation also is susceptible to misuse, with the potential to become a tool to maintain high prices, and to provide a legal mechanism to enforce a cartel's price.

The proposal for a competitive market is not an indictment against HACTL. Throughout most of its history, HACTL has been relatively successful in providing quality service and "holding the line" on its cargo rates. Between 1986 and 1989, for example, HACTL held its rates constant, bringing rates in real terms to a level 20 percent below those of 1976. (This policy abruptly changed with the construction of Terminal 2 because HACTL must fully recoup the building's costs prior to Kai Tak's closing in 1997.)[3] The company deserves serious consideration for a Chek Lap Kok license.

Singapore's Changi Airport illustrates the workability of competition under a duopoly system, showing that price or rate-of-return regulation probably would not be necessary at Chek Lap Kok. Both terminal operators, Singapore Air Terminal Services (SATS) and Changi International Airport Services (CIAS), are profitable and expanding ventures. Shippers have been so satisfied with the unregulated duopoly arrangement that they consistently rank both operators among the top three in Asia.

3. Apparently, HACTL had little choice but to increase rates nearly 30 percent annually for three consecutive years, to their current level of HK$0.98 per kilogram. However, disagreement exists about whether HACTL acted upon incentives to expand its profits through excessive investments in capital-intensive facilities. The tendency for regulated monopolies to expand their profits through excessive capitalization is sometimes referred to as the Averch-Johnson Effect and is the source of exhaustive economic debate.

5. How Should Terminal Operators Be Chosen?

The PAA should choose terminal operators on the strength of their proposals and financing plans. It should charge each terminal operator a flat annual license fee based on the amount of land used at Chek Lap Kok. This selection technique would have significant advantages over the "open tender" licensing scheme used at the Kwai Chung container port. An open tender system would favor those operators that expect to earn monopoly profits through market domination. A single company, or two closely allied companies, would be willing to bid more for a terminal license than two competitors. While an open tender system may provide greater revenues to the Airport Authority, these revenues are not real benefits to the local economy. They are merely transfers from consumers to the government, financed by higher terminal fees.

A misunderstanding about these issues is the basis for two common arguments against a competitive market for terminal services. One common argument is that competition would reduce the license fees that terminal operators are willing to pay. For reasons stated above, this is undoubtedly true: two competitors may be unwilling to pay the same license fees as a regulated monopolist, whose profits are assured. However, this is a flawed objection because license fees are not real benefits to the Hong Kong economy. Rather, they are merely transfers to the airport authority from local consumers and shippers. Another objection to awarding licenses to several terminal operators is that it would lead to higher capital costs. Some have voiced concern that investors will insist upon higher rates of return if their investments are subject to competition. However, the eagerness of five reputable entities to operate terminals at Chek Lap Kok contradicts this view, suggesting that low-cost financing will not be a problem.

As these facts show, the Provisional Airport Authority must enlist the services of several terminal operators if a major hub at Chek Lap Kok is to become a reality. It must adopt a market-oriented approach to give South China diversified and high-quality terminal services.

Chapter 4

Bilateral Treaties and Market Performance

Terminals are not the only problem facing the local cargo industry. The cumbersome bilateral process that regulates growth could be a serious deterrent to Chek Lap Kok's development into a major cargo hub. A review of the essential elements of the regulatory environment, the effects of the regulatory system on industry behavior, and its damaging effects on prices and innovation is provided below. The review illuminates the advantages of the proposal to overhaul regulatory policies for all-cargo flights, which is the focus of Chapter 5.

1. The Regulatory Environment

Airline services in Hong Kong are strictly controlled by government negotiated air service agreements. Following the precedent established by the United States and the United Kingdom at the "Bermuda I" conference in 1946, the Hong Kong government negotiates for various air service "freedoms" on behalf of its airlines:

- First freedoms are rights to fly over a country without landing.
- *Second freedoms* are rights to land in a country strictly for technical reasons, such as refueling.
- *Third freedoms* are rights to pick up cargo in a carrier's home country and transport it to a foreign country.
- *Fourth freedoms* are rights to pick up cargo in a foreign country and transport it to the carrier's home country.
- *Fifth freedoms* are rights to carry cargo between two foreign countries.

This framework has become the standard model used by governments worldwide for bilateral discussions of air passenger and cargo services. The system is used not only to control the access of foreign carriers to a country, but to control the capacities of their flights and the market share of local airlines. Bilateral agreements prescribe the particular airports that carriers can serve, the size of the aircraft that they can operate, and the frequency of service that they can provide. Third and fourth freedoms are the most commonly negotiated item. (A combination of third and fourth freedoms is sometimes referred to as a "sixth" freedom.) For example, Hong Kong has negotiated third and fourth freedoms covering most major foreign destinations and has designated Cathay Pacific Airlines to exercise these freedoms.

As carriers begin to compete on a global scale, fifth freedoms are becoming an increasingly pivotal negotiating issue. European and North American carriers are pressuring their governments to negotiate fifth freedom rights, which would allow the carriers to serve lucrative inter-Asia markets. For example, UPS and Federal Express are eager to join U.S. passenger airlines in providing services from Hong Kong to Toyko, but their governments have not yet attained the prerequisite fifth freedom rights.

After the various freedoms are negotiated, they are compiled in a comprehensive "air service agreement." Until recently, the United Kingdom controlled all air service agreements involving Hong Kong. It combined Great Britain's air service agreements with Hong Kong's. Therefore, if a foreign carrier sought to add a new flight to Hong Kong, its government first had to negotiate for such a right with the British — an arrangement that rendered Hong Kong's air cargo industry vulnerable to the vagaries of British diplomacy. The British have historically favored restrictive air service agreements as a means of protecting its carriers. They also are alleged to have offered overseas airlines the right to fly to Hong Kong as a bargaining chip to gain British carriers new opportunities on North Atlantic routes.

Some maintain that British insensitivity toward Hong Kong led it to compromise the interests of Hong Kong carriers with the signing of the U.K.-China Air Service Agreement. This agreement, signed in 1980, grants Chinese airlines extensive rights to fly to Hong Kong without giving Hong Kong's carriers reciprocal rights, thus hampering the expansion of Hong Kong carriers onto the mainland. Hong Kong officials were able to participate only informally in these critical bilateral negotiations.

Hong Kong's air service agreements now fall under the exclusive jurisdiction of the Economic Services Branch of the Hong Kong government. Under the provisions of the Sino-British Joint Declaration, the Hong Kong government has the authority to separate Hong Kong from the old British-negotiated agreements. New bilateral treaties between Hong Kong and most of the 24 affected foreign governments are already in effect. (These treaties are sometimes shrouded in secrecy: The Hong Kong government, unlike many other countries, has chosen not to make them available for public inspection.) The Hong Kong government has been unable to establish new agreements with two countries, the United States and Japan.

If no agreements are reached by 1997, the existing treaties with the United States and Japan will expire and negotiations for revised ones will have to proceed with the input of the Chinese government. This means that Beijing will have the power to veto all future air service pacts. However, considering China's recent efforts to improve the access of foreign airlines to its airports, there is good reason to believe that it will be disposed to more liberal bilateral agreements.[1]

Hong Kong uses another unit of its government, the Air Transport Licensing Authority, to determine which local carriers can exercise the various freedoms negotiated as part of an air service agreement. This authority, consisting of at least three officials appointed by the governor, has the power to approve or disapprove all requests by local carriers for new services. It holds public or private hearings before awarding new routes, and considers issues such as market demand,

1. Joint Declaration also stipulates that Chinese carriers have unlimited access to Hong Kong airports after 1997. Chinese carriers will be able to regard Hong Kong as a domestic destination and serve international routes from Hong Kong without first obtaining fifth freedom rights. Hong Kong's inability to fully control its skies may complicate its efforts to establish a consistent aviation policy.

the applicant's aircraft and financial resources, and the general interest of the public.

An Anti-Competitive Device

The complex regulatory process described above is not used merely to oversee the growth of air services, it is used as an anti-competitive device. Four local policies are particularly damaging to competition among cargo carriers:

- In bilateral negotiations, Hong Kong typically rejects requests for new third and fourth freedoms (i.e., the right to fly between a carrier's home country and Hong Kong) unless local carriers want to expand service in the applicant's home country. Although this "exchange" policy is not unusual in international aviation, it is a particularly formidable barrier to entry into the Hong Kong market because the dominant local carrier, Cathay Pacific, is unprepared for or uninterested in expanding service on many key routes.
- Attempts by foreign counties to negotiate fifth freedom rights (i.e., the right for an airline to carry cargo between Hong Kong to another foreign country) are systematically rejected. Although European and North American carriers have successfully negotiated rights to expand services from other Asian nations, Hong Kong's unyielding position has left them little room for compromise.
- Only one locally based airline (generally Cathay Pacific) is designated by the Air Transport Licensing Authority to serve the most important routes from Hong Kong, despite provisions in bilateral negotiations that allow for the designation of multiple carriers. This policy is inconsistent with the policies of virtually all major exporting countries, including Japan, Taiwan, South Korea, and the United States, which give several carriers the authority to serve their most important routes. (For example, Japan routinely authorizes both Japan Air Lines and Nippon Cargo Airlines to serve important routes.)
- Week-by-week limits on the amount of cargo that charter operators can haul are occasionally imposed by the Air Transport Licensing Authority. This policy serves to protect local carriers, most

notably Cathay Pacific Airlines and Air Hong Kong, from seasonal competitors, such as Cargolux Airlines and Martinair.

Although using these types of regulatory actions to protect incumbent local airlines once was a common practice in international trade, governments worldwide are moving to liberalize air service policies. Throughout Europe, North America, and Asia, regulatory barriers are being scaled back, particularly for cargo services. Five developments are particularly notable: (1) Singapore, South Korea, the Netherlands, Taiwan, and the Philippines offer carriers from many foreign countries virtually unrestricted access to their airports; (2) Greece, Italy, Spain, and the United States have taken steps to remove cargo services from bilateral treaties dominated by passenger issues (Martin, 1991); (3) the European Community recently took a bold step, agreeing to give the airlines of its member states unlimited authority to provide air service between any two points within that continent; (4) The United States, Canada, and Mexico are drawing up plans to give airlines unrestricted access to airports throughout the continent as part of the North American Free Trade Agreement; (5) the British, once a strong advocate of protectionism, are considering an "open skies" treaty with the United States. In this changing environment, Hong Kong's defensive and unyielding position in some of its bilateral negotiations has rightfully earned it a reputation as a militant adversary of free trade in aviation services.

Hong Kong's staunch negotiating stance is said to be necessary because of capacity constraints at Kai Tak Airport, which make expansion difficult to accommodate. Local behaviour, however, is inconsistent with this explanation. For example, these capacity problems cannot explain the government's refused to granting fifth freedom rights on flights already in operation, such as those daily freighters operated by foreign carriers between Hong Kong and Japan and Taiwan. Nor can they justify the government's refusal to consider more liberal agreements after new parking bays are completed at Kai Tak, which will partially alleviate capacity shortages. Most importantly, Kai Tak's capacity problems cannot explain the government's unwillingness to approve more liberal agreements for services commencing after the opening of Chek Lap Kok. The persistence of restrictive bilateral agreements suggests that Hong Kong's primary motive is to protect existing local airlines.

2. Industry Behaviour under Regulation

A review of some recent developments in the local air cargo industry shows how restrictive air service agreements are heightening the political orientation of airlines. They are encouraging non-market competition, such as legal confrontations, lobbying, and various forms of diplomatic positioning, to supplant vigorous market competition. In this politicized environment, the decisions of cargo airlines are frequently justified not on the basis of their market value to shippers and consumers, but on the basis of their ability to affect the regulatory process.

A principal beneficiary of the existing regulatory structure is Cathay Pacific Airlines. Founded in 1946, Cathay Pacific has grown to become the world's tenth largest carrier of cargo, handling more than 1,000 tonnes daily. It is Hong Kong's only local carrier with authority to provide scheduled service between the territory and key commercial centers, including London, Paris, Seoul, Taipei, and Tokyo. Cathay has a tremendous stake in the preservation of the existing regulatory system, which has helped it become one of the world's most profitable and credit worthy airlines.[2] Cargo service, which accounts for about 20 percent of the company's revenues, is an integral part of its profitability.

The regulatory impediments to competition offer Cathay lucrative and relatively low-risk opportunities for expansion. Cathay plans to greatly expand its cargo capacity by adding three additional Boeing

2. In 1992, Cathay earned more than HK$3.2 billion in profits on revenue turnover of HK$23.3 billion — a profit margin of 13.7 percent. During 1991, the carrier reported the third highest net income of any member of the International Air Transport Association. Its profits were surpassed only by Korean Airlines and Singapore Airlines. Cathay Pacific earns an estimated 85 percent of its cargo revenues with its fleet of 45 widebody aircraft, including 27 Boeing 747s and 18 Lockheed L1011 TriStars.

747s, 11 Boeing 777s, and 10 Airbus A330s to its fleet. These planes will support Cathay's four recently acquired Boeing 747 freighters that are being used to serve Dubai, Frankfurt, London, Los Angeles, Melbourne, Paris, Sydney, and Tokyo. The carrier also is planning to build upon its successful cargo mini-hubs in Frankfurt and Paris, where it coordinates flight schedules with highway distribution systems.

Although Cathay is the only local carrier with the legal authority to provide scheduled cargo service to numerous North American cities, it remains relatively non-aggressive in this market. Its only North American freighter service, which operates three times a week to Los Angeles, gives it less than 10 percent of the U.S. market. Although Cathay actively promotes it by offering attractive prices and low-cost ground delivery to many U.S. cities, this service remains unprofitable. Cathay's willingness to accept these losses may have a regulatory motive: The service effectively pre-empts other local carriers, such as Air Hong Kong, from acquiring the regulatory authority to launch scheduled service and gain a foothold in this expanding market.

Regulatory issues are also affecting the decisions of Cathay's parent company, Swire Pacific. (Swire Pacific's presence is felt in virtually all aspects of Hong Kong aviation, including catering, ground handling, terminals, maintenance, and air services.) Such issues helped motivate Swire to have Cathay Pacific, its subsidiary, acquire a 35 percent equity stake in Dragonair, Hong Kong's second largest passenger airline. This transaction allowed Dragonair to take over Cathay's existing services to the mainland, including its Hong Kong-Beijing and Hong Kong-Shanghai flights, and to enlarge Dragonair's route network to 18 Asian destinations, including 12 in China. Dragonair's emphasis on Chinese routes is politically expedient: It enables Cathay to abandon its awkward negotiations with the Chinese, who have repeatedly denied it opportunities to expand on the mainland, and eliminates Cathay's need to compete head-to-head with Chinese carriers on politically sensitive routes (Bowring, 1992a).

Cathay's difficulties with China were partially the result of the

U.K.-China Air Service Agreement, which limits the share of Chinese traffic available to Hong Kong carriers through 1997. But Cathay's problems were exacerbated by its British ownership. Although the Joint Declaration does not explicitly prevent the foreign ownership of Hong Kong's airlines, some Chinese negotiators apparently did not look favorably toward Cathay for this reason. (Chinese negotiators may remember that Cathay was accused of denying high-paying cockpit crew positions to people of Chinese ethnicity — an exclusionary policy that did not apply to low-paying flight attendant positions (Bowring, 1992a).) Due to the vagaries of the regulatory process, Swire Pacific's British investors may need to sell part of their stake in Cathay to local or mainland interests if the airline is to aggressively expand onto the mainland (Westlake, 1992).[3]

The politically charged regulatory climate between Hong Kong and China may help explain the growing equity relationship between Chinese entities and local airlines. Keenly aware of the importance of having Chinese stockholders, Cathay and Dragonair stand to benefit from three stock transactions that were consummated recently:

- The China Trust and Investment Corporation (CITIC) Pacific recently acquired a 38-percent stake in Dragonair and a 12.5-percent stake in Cathay Pacific. CITIC Pacific is a Hong Kong listed investment holding company controlled by China's State Council.
- The China Travel Service (CTS), which participates in regulatory activities in China, recently acquired a 5-percent stake in Cathay Pacific.
- The China National Aviation Corporation (CNAC) recently

3. Dragonair's new routes, its partnership with Cathay, and its more favorable image in China are beginning to pay dividends for Swire. In 1991, for example, Dragonair began using Cathay as its general sales agent, or its marketing unit, for all cargo originating in Hong Kong. This arrangement gives Dragonair access to Cathay's CUBIC system, a cargo reservation system that provides instant information on space availability and, in the eyes of shippers, makes the two airlines effectively a single operator. The two airlines are collectively building Hong Kong into one of the largest carrgo hubs in Asia (Bowring, 1992a).

acquired a 5-percent stake in Cathay Pacific from the Hong Kong Bank, a deal the carrier pushed hard to make possible.

Although these transactions give Chinese institutions only minority stakes in the two Hong Kong airlines, they give the carriers additional leverage in future Sino-Hong Kong negotiations. Especially advantageous are their affiliations with CNAC, which will improve Cathay's ability to acquire traffic rights within China. As the general sales agent in Hong Kong for the Civil Aviation Administration of China (CAAC) and the holding company for Air China, China Eastern Airlines and China Southern Airlines, CNAC has much clout in determining internal aviation policy. The authority of this Chinese entity is likely to diminish in upcoming years as its regulatory and business activities are split. Its presence, however, will be felt in all important aviation-related decisions.

While the regulatory system is working to the advantage of Cathay, it is hampering the growth of Air Hong Kong. Hong Kong's only all-cargo airline, Air Hong Kong, made inauspicious beginnings by initiating charter service in 1987 with a single, aging Boeing 707 aircraft. Since then, the carrier has publicized its ambitious plans for regularly scheduled flights to Europe and North America. Shunning the caution of Cathay Pacific, Air Hong Kong aspires to quickly establish itself as a global competitor.

Air Hong Kong's expansion has been supported by Dr. Stanley Ho of Shun Tak Enterprises of Macao, who acquired a 50-percent stake in the carrier in 1989. His financial support allowed the carrier to initiate scheduled all-cargo service between Hong Kong and Manchester, England, and gain a 30-percent share of the British market. In 1991, Air Hong Kong began service to Brussels. That same year, it became one of Hong Kong's 12 largest general cargo airlines.

Air Hong Kong's desire to grow rapidly is awkward for Cathay Pacific because it draws attention to the older carrier's lack of interest in new traffic rights. Before Air Hong Kong announced its growth plans, for example, Cathay Pacific expressed little interest in cargo operations to North America. Only after Air Hong Kong filed its application to begin freighter service to Los Angeles did Cathay Pacific exercise its long-standing but unused right to operate freighters on the route. This pre-emptive action was successful: The Hong Kong government subsequently denied Air Hong Kong the authority to directly serve Los Angeles, a move which highlighted the carrier's difficulties in acquiring valuable new routes.

The regulatory process is also thwarting Air Hong Kong's expansion into other markets. In November 1991, for example, Air Hong Kong took a bold step with its application to serve 55 new destinations worldwide. Cathay Pacific vigorously opposed the application, questioning Air Hong Kong's ability to effectively serve such a sprawling route network. Also working against the proposal was Air Hong Kong's aging fleet, consisting of only two Boeing 707 aircraft and several converted Boeing 747 planes (*Shippers Today*, 1992). After much publicized debate, the carrier received rights to serve 14 additional destinations — all less important to Cathay Pacific than to charter airlines and foreign passenger carriers. The Air Transport Licensing Authority, with few exceptions, held true to its one-airline-per-route policy, thus preventing the upstart from launching scheduled service to important destinations such as Seoul, Taipei and Tokyo.[4]

The regulatory structure is similarly limiting the expansion of foreign carriers into Hong Kong. The inability of foreign governments to negotiate fifth freedom rights not only prevents carriers from adding new flights from Hong Kong to other Asian cities, it prevents

4. With its newly acquired routes, Air Hong Kong has the authority to enlarge its operation to 31 cities. However, because many of these routes are of only secondary importance, the additions may not be enough to save the carrier, which has been unprofitable since its inception. Recognizing that Air Hong Kong's demise would generate significant negative publicity or, worse still, lead to the entry of an even stronger competitor, Cathay Pacific has reassured anxious investors that it would not engage in predatory pricing or undertake special marketing efforts to add to the smaller carrier's troubles. But a bitter relationship continues between these rivals, and Cathay Pacific remains unwilling to cooperate in efforts to strengthen Air Hong Kong. The larger carrier has expressed little interest in integrating Air Hong Kong's flights into its hub operation, which may be necessary for the upstart to survive (Bowring, 1992a).

them from carrying cargo on many existing flights that link Hong Kong to Asian points as continuations of North American or European flights. For example, Lufthansa is not permitted to handle freight on flights between Hong Kong and Bangkok; UPS, Federal Express and Northwest Airlines are not permitted to carry intra-Asian cargo on their freighters linking Hong Kong with Japan. The absence of fifth freedom rights also requires freighters to operate largely empty to Taiwan and Singapore. Eager to expand in the Pacific Rim, foreign carriers of express and general cargo are diverting their energies from providing new air services to lobbying for additional traffic rights. One carrier, Federal Express, even commissioned a study to draw attention to the issue.

Because of the importance of American carriers in international cargo services, the content of the air service agreement between Hong Kong and the United States will have major implications for the region. The United States has asked Hong Kong to triple its fifth freedom rights, increasing service from 21 to 70 flights per week. The United States also has requested that its airlines be permitted to serve Hong Kong from additional gateways (i.e., cities) on the U.S. mainland. (Service currently is provided from Seattle, San Francisco and Los Angeles.)

Several rounds of unsuccessful negotiations, ending in mid-1992, led to a stalemate. The United States claims that Hong Kong is engaging in protectionism, and Hong Kong maintains that it is only acting in its best interest. Hong Kong also contends that the United States has failed to offer sufficient concessions to justify a new agreement. The stalemate has virtually halted the increase in cargo flights between the countries, directly affecting six of the world's 15 largest cargo airlines.

Foreign carriers are voicing concern that regulatory policies will deny them the opportunity to develop Chek Lap Kok as a cargo hub. Due to the sluggish, unresponsive nature of the bilateral process and opposition of local airlines, however, there is little chance that these concerns will lead to more liberal bilateral treaties any time soon. An environment of mistrust and suspicion prevails at the bargaining table.

3. Problems in Market Performance

When a political process supplants market competition, one discernable effect is a high level of market concentration, which puts upward pressure on prices. Another effect is dampened innovation and investment, which denies local shippers access to many services.

Market Concentration and High Prices

Hong Kong's policies are stifling competition on inter-Asia routes, where only a select group of carriers have the legal authority to handle cargo (Table 4.1). Because local and foreign carriers have repeatedly been denied the regulatory authority to serve these routes, an oligopoly prevails. Three carriers handle 98 percent of the cargo between Hong Kong and Seoul, 93 percent between Hong Kong and Taipei, 90 percent between Hong Kong and Tokyo, and 87 percent between Hong Kong and Bangkok. Between Hong Kong and Singapore, three carriers handle 86 percent of the cargo. In each case, the market share held by a single carrier exceeds 35 percent.

Longer-haul routes are generally less concentrated. Shippers of North American cargo may choose any of eight airlines serving that continent directly, or four carriers using intermediate hubs in South

Table 4.1. Market Concentration on Asian Routes

Destination	Three Carrier Market Share*	Carriers
Bangkok	87%	CI, CX, TG
Seoul	96%	CX, KE
Singapore	86%	CI, CX, SQ
Taipei	92%	CI, CX, JL
Tokyo	90%	CX, JL, KZ

* Based on 1991 tonnage. Includes direct flights only.

Carrier codes: China Airlines (CI), Cathay Pacific Airlines (CX), Korean Airlines (KE), Japan Airlines (JL), Nippon Cargo Airlines (KZ), Singapore Airlines (SQ), Thai Airlines (TG).

Korea, Japan, or Taiwan, where carriers have the legal authority to handle transpacific cargo from Hong Kong. Similarly, services to Europe are provided by more than 10 carriers. Nevertheless, price competition is sometimes thwarted on these routes, such as the one between Chicago and Hong Kong, where carriers have been unsuccessful in obtaining the necessary rights to launch nonstop service.

The small number of carriers offering all cargo "freighter" service from Hong Kong to major Asian cities serves as testimony to the anti-competitive effects of Hong Kong's policies (Table 4.2). Shippers in Hong Kong have fewer alternatives for larger shipments to Asia's dominant cargo destinations, including Bangkok, Singapore, Taipei, and Tokyo, than do shippers located in other Asian cities. For example, while three airlines provide freighter services to Tokyo from Hong Kong, five airlines provide them to Tokyo from Taipei. Similarly, nonstop freighter service to Singapore is provided by only one airline from Hong Kong, but services are provided by three airlines from Taipei and four airlines from Tokyo. An even greater discrepancy exists for services to Bangkok, where eight airlines operate freighters from Singapore (although some operate only once per week), three operate them from Taipei, and five operate them from Tokyo, but only one operates them from Hong Kong. These differences are striking considering that, with the exception of Tokyo, the Hong Kong cargo market is much larger than those of these other cities.

These entry barriers have undesirable effects. Earlier studies warn that prices at heavily concentrated airports are significantly higher than those at less concentrated airports (Borenstein, 1988; Bailey, 1985). In the U.S. market, for example, entry and price controls resulted in prices 18 percent higher than those of the current deregulated market (Morrison and Winston, 1990). Even the mere threat of entry, or the possibility that a new entrant would challenge (i.e., "contest") incumbent operators, could enhance price competition. Studies show that airlines are encouraged to keep prices low to deter would-be competitors from entering the market (Morrison and Winston, 1987).

In Hong Kong, entry barriers are driving prices up to artificially

Table 4.2. Scheduled Freighter Service

	Number of Carriers			
	To Bangkok	To Singapore	To Taipei	To Tokyo
Bangkok		2 (KE, TG)	3 (CI, FM, TL)	3 (JL, KZ, TL)
Hong Kong	1 (CX)	1 (LD)	3 (CI, CX, NW)	3 (KZ, JL, CX)
Singapore	8 (*)	4	3 (CI, FM, SQ, TN)	(KE, JL, NW)
Taipei	3 (CU, TL, FM)	3 (CI, SQ, TN)		5 (CI, CX, FM, LG, NW)
Tokyo	5 (AF, FM, KZ, SV, TV)	4 (JL, KZ, NW, FM)	5 (CI, CX, EF, FM, NW)	

* CI, JL, KE, KZ, FM, NW, SQ, TL.
Carrier codes: Air Hong Kong (LD), Air France (AF), China Airlines (CI), Cathay Pacific Airlines (CX), Federal Express(FM), Haiti Trans Air (TV), Japan Airlines (JL), Korean Airlines (KE), Saudi Arabian Airlines (SV), Singapore Airlines (SQ), Thai Airlines (TG), TNT Express Worldwide (TN), Trans-Mediterranean Airlines (TL).
Sources: OAG *Air Cargo Guide* (January, 1993); *Traffic World* (1993).

high levels. A sample of the prices published in the June 1992 issue of *The Air Cargo Tariff*, a comprehensive source of air cargo prices, shows that Hong Kong's shippers pay more than other shippers for comparable air services. The sample consists of prices in 125 city pairs involving six Asian destinations — Bangkok, Hong Kong, Kuala Lumpur, Manila, Singapore, and Taipei. These cities are in close proximity to Hong Kong, but have more pro-competitive policies. (Cargo prices from Japan are excluded from the sample because the country's aviation policies, like Hong Kong's, are highly restrictive.)

Published prices, of course, are not always completely accurate barometers of actual prices because most air carriers offer significant discounts. However, it is reasonable to assume that carriers offer consistent discounts across all flight origins and destinations.

(According to Asian freight forwarders, the average discount is approximately 30 percent.) This simplifying assumption offers a best-case scenario for Hong Kong, considering that many local forwarders reported smaller discounts in Hong Kong than in neighboring countries.

The regression model used to compare prices is summarized in the Appendix. The results show that shippers in Hong Kong pay prices averaging HK$4.31 more per kilogram than those in the other cities, after adjusting for flight distance and market size. The effects of these price differences under two hypothetical scenarios are shown in Figure 4.1. For a 45-kilogram parcel shipped over a low-volume, 2,000-mile route, shippers in Hong Kong can expect to pay HK$30.80

Figure 4.1. Average Price of Air Cargo Service

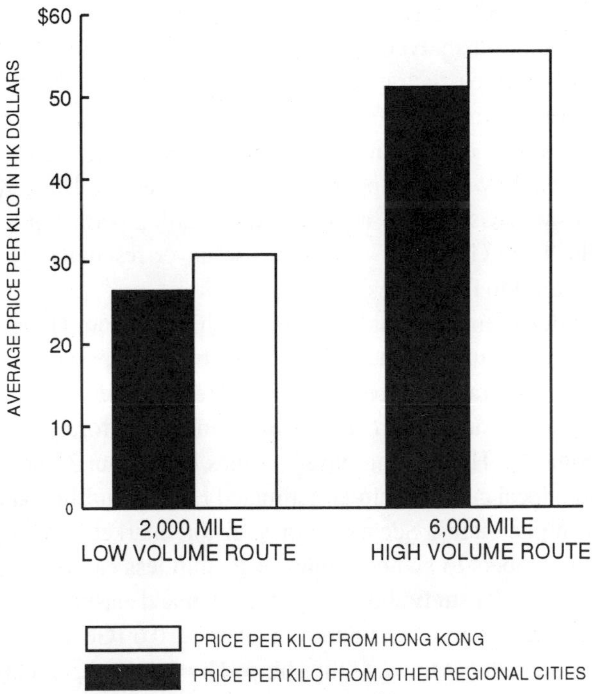

Based on prices reported in the *Air Cargo Tariff*, August 1992.

per kilogram. For the same parcel over an equivalent route, shippers in cities with more competitive aviation policies can expect to pay only HK$26.50 — about 16 percent less. Over a low-volume, 4,000-mile route, shippers from Hong Kong can expect to pay HK$55.40 per kilogram, compared with HK$51.10 for shippers in more competitive locations — a difference of 8 percent.

For the average shipment, Hong Kong shippers pay at least 10 percent more than those in other cities. Less than half of this price difference can be attributed to high aeronautical fees at Kai Tak airport. These fees account for only about 12 percent to 15 percent of a cargo airline's total costs (Yue, 1992). On average, Hong Kong's aeronautical fees are no more than 25 percent higher than other regional airports. In fact, Hong Kong's fees are much lower than those of Singapore (Bowring, 1992a). (A typical landing fee for a Boeing 747 is HK$12,000 in Hong Kong and HK$16,000 in Singapore.) Thus, the higher-than-average fees at Kai Tak can plausibly explain no more than three to four percentage points of the estimated 10 percent average price difference. The absence of competition is responsible for, at a minimum, six and seven percentage points of the premiums paid by local shippers. The upward trend in Hong Kong's cargo rates was hastened by an across-the-board, 7-percent price hike during the 1990 Gulf War — an increase never rescinded despite a subsequent fall in fuel prices.

The price premiums paid by regional shippers from Hong Kong, conservatively estimated at 5 percent, have two important implications. First, they transfer an estimated HK$698 million annually from shippers and consumers to cargo airlines, including foreign carriers. Considering that Hong Kong-based airlines hold about 35 percent of the market, local carriers gain an estimated HK$244 million annually from the higher fares. Secondly, they distort market behavior, encouraging shippers to switch modes or to ship less cargo altogether. Based on an earlier study showing that the demand elasticity for Hong Kong's air cargo services is approximately — 0.6 (Gellman, 1990), the price hike reduces the quantity shipped by at least 3 percent. With a few simplifying assumptions, it can be concluded that the "dead-weight loss" — the net welfare loss borne by those not shipping air cargo because of the price premium — is almost HK$11 million annually.[5]

The elimination of entry barriers for cargo carriers would help close the price gap between Hong Kong and neighboring airports. The above calculations suggest that this policy would benefit the South China region by HK$464 million annually. (It would provide HK$698 million in benefits to shippers and consumers of existing air cargo plus HK$11 million in benefits to shippers and consumers of newly generated cargo, and result in HK$244 million in lost profits to local carriers.)

Reduced Innovation

The entry barriers are also discouraging innovation and improvements to service quality. Research shows that consumers suffer more from the reduced service quality caused by entry barriers than from the artificially high prices (Winston and Morrison, 1986). Not only do they affect the ability of carriers to effectively manage the tradeoff between service quality and price (Keeler, 1972), they prevent carriers from modifying their route systems to facilitate more convenient flight connections (Carlton, Landes, and Posner, 1980; Johnson, 1985).

Regulatory controls are denying Hong Kong shippers access to nonstop air service on many routes. Hong Kong is home to two of Asia's three largest markets without any regularly scheduled freighter service, Hong Kong-Manila and Hong Kong-Osaka. Hong Kong

5. These calculations are based on a 5-percent local price premium and annual air cargo revenues of HK$13.95 billion, at an average price of HK$0.0175 million per ton. Based on a demand elasticity of –0.6 and throughput of 800,000 tonnes, the quantity of cargo shipped is estimated to fall by 3 percent, or 24,000 tonnes. The "deadweight loss" calculation is based on a linear demand curve. Under this scenario, the average deadweight loss will be exactly one-half of the price increase, or about HK$0.00044 million per ton. Multiplying 24,000 tonnes by HK$0.00044 million yields a total deadweight loss of HK$10.5 million.

also is falling behind Singapore in the development of EDI systems, which could improve speed and reliability. Most importantly, as shown in Chapter 2, entry barriers stand in the way of Chek Lap Kok's development as a major express cargo hub.

Chapter 5

A Proposal for Growth

The suggested proposal to overhaul the regulatory system for air cargo services calls for the Hong Kong government's Economic Service Branch to take three initiatives:

- Unilaterally grant a limited number of fifth freedom rights to all-cargo flights serving Kai Tak, and grant unlimited rights for future all-cargo services to Chek Lap Kok.
- Support efforts to negotiate air cargo rights through a multilateral process, such as the General Agreement on Tariffs and Trade (GATT).
- Allocate a portion of additional capacity at Kai Tak Airport for all-cargo flights serving Asian destinations.

The proposal also calls for the Air Transport Licensing Authority to take one action:

- Designate two or more local carriers to operate all-cargo services from Hong Kong where permitted in existing bilateral treaties.

1. Justification

The existing bilateral approach was shown in Chapter 4 to shift decision-making from the marketplace to the non-market arena, encouraging carriers to use lobbying efforts and political influence as a surrogate for effective market performance. The bilateral approach is also susceptible to retaliation, protectionism, and the vagaries of international diplomacy.

As a preliminary step to removing air cargo from this restrictive system, the proposal calls for the Civil Aeronautics Division of the Economic Services Branch to unilaterally offer fifth freedom rights for five to ten daily all-cargo flights between Kai Tak and other major

Asian destinations. Although night time curfews and inadequate terminal services will prevent the development of a full-fledged express hub operation at Kai Tak, this action would demonstrate Hong Kong's commitment to becoming a viable hub candidate and allow potential hub operators to gain a stronger foothold in the South China market. This action would also improve efficiency by allowing carriers to carry cargo on flights already operated between Hong Kong and other Asian destinations as continuations of their services to Europe and North America. A system of competitive bidding would be used if several carriers simultaneously requested these traffic rights.

Local carriers would also be given new opportunities to participate in the expanding regional market. The Air Transport Licensing Authority would authorize a second local carrier to operate all-cargo flights to important destinations where permitted by bilateral treaties. Air Hong Kong appears to be an eager candidate to launch scheduled service between Hong Kong and Los Angeles, Seoul, Taipei, and Tokyo.

Granting additional traffic rights to operators of all-cargo flights will not result in substantial benefit unless these operators are able to land and park their aircraft at congested Kai Tak airport. Parking space for widebody aircraft remains in particularly short supply. However, these shortages will soon be temporarily alleviated.[1] To assure that new airport capacity is put to good use, the proposal calls for a portion of it to be designated for new entrants providing all-cargo flight services in highly concentrated Asian markets.

As Chek Lap Kok's opening and reunification with China draw near, Hong Kong must take an even bolder step. The proposal calls for the government's Economic Services Branch to offer unlimited traffic rights, including fifth freedom rights, for all-cargo flights commenc-

1. Four parking bays for Boeing 747-size aircraft were recently completed and 11 parking bays for widebody aircraft on reclaimed land in Kowloon Bay have been put on a "fast track" process for completion in early 1994. Engineering efforts to tighten the spacing of departures at Kai Tak also are expected to improve capacity prior to 1997.

ing after the new airport's opening. This policy would remove all-cargo flights from the politicized negotiating process that is currently dominated by passenger-related concerns. (It has successfully been used by Greece and Spain to break bargaining impasses with the United States.) The policy would virtually eliminate the risk of regulatory obstacles inhibiting Chek Lap Kok's development as a cargo hub and would allow carriers to confidently make the investments necessary to successfully launch a major hub operation in 1997.

Although it behooves Hong Kong to consider extending this action to passenger flights, the proposal is limited to all-cargo flights for reasons of political expediency. Considering incumbent carriers' opposition to liberalization, it is unlikely that the unwieldy bilateral structure for passenger flights will be overhauled in the foreseeable future. Including passenger services in the proposal could needlessly stall governmental action. However, because the belly cargo services provided in conjunction with passenger flights are vital to the region's future, Hong Kong should support efforts to remove belly services from the bilateral process as well. The proposal urges Hong Kong to support a multilateral negotiating process, such as the General Agreement on Tariffs and Trade (GATT), for all air cargo services. The European Community and South American nations already have taken steps to arrange for a multilateral process for cargo services, and several southeastern nations, including Brunei, Indonesia, Malaysia, Singapore, and Thailand, have begun moving in this direction as well (Martin, 1991). Hong Kong cannot afford to stand idly by and place the future of Chek Lap Kok's cargo industry in the hands of the unwieldy and unresponsive negotiating process that prevails today.

Ultimately, the Economic Service Branch should take note of the growing body of evidence showing that the bilateral process is hampering the efficiency of all types of air services, including passenger services. An earlier study by Kai-Sun Kwong (1988) illustrates the problems associated with the restrictive bilateral process for Hong Kong's passenger services. Singapore, South Korea, Taiwan, and The Philippines all have adopted policies that give both passenger and cargo airlines considerable freedom in establishing new services to their airports, and could serve as excellent role models for Hong Kong.

2. Opposition to Liberalization

The merits of the above proposal can be best understood against the backdrop of the flawed arguments used to justify the existing system. Those opposed to moving away from the existing bilateral policy often cite five arguments in its defense: (1) it serves to transfer wealth to Hong Kong; (2) it helps local airlines exploit economies of scope; (3) it fosters external benefits by strengthening the local airline industry; (4) it stabilizes prices; and (5) it allows Hong Kong to negotiate strategically for reciprocal benefits.

(1) Transferring Wealth to Hong Kong

Restrictive bilateral treaties are believed by some to benefit the regional economy by allowing local air carriers to take advantage of Hong Kong's favorable location and earn supernormal profits (i.e., "rents"). Because Hong Kong is considered such a critical transfer point for Chinese exports, advocates recommend that Hong Kong take advantage of its position through the monopolistic pricing of aviation services. By limiting the supply of cargo services, restrictive air service agreements are seen as a tool to drive up prices. Because overseas buyers have little choice but to pay premium prices, the price increases are viewed as a way to transfer wealth from foreign countries to Hong Kong's airlines.

Superficially, this argument is appealing. Cathay Pacific has earned large profits in recent years, just as proponents of monopoly pricing would suggest. Moreover, many in Hong Kong adamantly believe that governmental policy should defend local carriers and that the adverse effects of these higher prices on the local economy are trivial.[2] Unfortunately, however, Hong Kong cannot realistically benefit from such a strategy. Buyers of South China products have

---

2. One official, for example, recently commented, "There really is not a case for sacrificing the specific legitimate interests of local airlines for some vaguely defined greater benefit for the Hong Kong economy" (Cathay Pacific Airlines, 1992).

increasingly attractive alternatives to shipping through Hong Kong, denying the territory the ability to pass on local price increase to those overseas. In fact, considering the high elasticity of demand for air cargo service (Gellman, 1990), local production apparently declines significantly when air cargo prices increase.

Another problem with the current strategy is that it assumes incorrectly that most of the additional profits earned by air carriers provide direct benefits to the Hong Kong economy. Because 65 percent of Hong Kong's air cargo is handled by foreign airlines, most of these profits are "exported" to overseas investors. In fact, Hong Kong's largest local carrier, Cathay Pacific Airlines, is largely owned by foreign interests. (British investors' stake in Cathay Pacific is so great that U.S. negotiators had to make special provisions in bilateral negotiations to allow it to retain its status as a local Hong Kong carrier after 1997).

A few simple calculations illustrate the problems associated with this argument. The barriers to competition were shown early to increase the annual profits of local carriers by about HK$244 million. Because local investors have a legal claim to at most 33 percent of these profits, they effectively earn HK$80 million. If we optimistically assume that three-fourths of the industry's price increases could be passed on to foreign consumers, then local businesses would incur additional costs of about HK$174 million per year due to the policy.[3] Under this optimistic scenario, the net effect of the policy is a loss of HK$94 million annually (HK$80 million minus HK$174 million) for Hong Kong.

The negative effects of the policy are exacerbated by other factors. Most notably, high prices suppress traffic, which hurts manufacturing and airport revenues — funds critical for financing the Chek Lap Kok project. They also negatively affect ground handling and terminal services, both very profitable local ventures.

3. These calculations are based on a 5 percent price premium and total annual revenues for air cargo operators of approximately HK$14 billion. They assume that local shippers bear 25 percent of this 5 percent price increase.

(2) Exploiting Economies of Scope

Some believe that trade agreements protecting local airlines are necessary to put them on a more even economic footing with foreign producers. If economies of scope exist in the production of air services, then airlines can lower their average costs by simultaneously producing many different products. (Economies of scope are similar to economies of scale, but emphasize the number of products, such as the number of routes, that carriers offer, rather than the absolute size of their operations.) Restrictive air service agreements are seen as a tool to allow local airlines to expand at the expense of foreign airlines, thus giving them a competitive advantage.[4]

This defense of the existing policy is flawed for two reasons. First, the advantages bestowed upon Hong Kong's carriers through trade restrictions come at the expense of foreign carriers. Therefore, foreign governments have good reason to retaliate if Hong Kong adopts protectionist policies. This creates an environment of mistrust that politicizes the air cargo marketplace, inhibiting its expansion. Second, efficiency often suffers when foreign carriers are denied the opportunity to expand. On many routes, foreign airlines have strong comparative advantages over local carriers. Policies aimed at boosting market share prevent the expansion of the most technically efficient carriers, causing higher prices than would exist under a free trade arrangement.

The comparative advantages of foreign carriers are especially important in the North American market, where traffic is scattered among 60 to 80 major destinations. For express services to expand

4. Airline executives in Hong Kong often stress the importance of economies of scope. Managers at Air Hong Kong, for example, know the airline's small route network denies it the "critical mass" necessary to be profitable and renders it more vulnerable to mechanical and weather-related problems. Similarly, Dragonair's managers recognize that the marketing affiliation with larger Cathay Pacific is critical because it enlarges the range of its services. These circumstances have led some to conclude that bilateral negotiations should be used to limit the expansion of foreign carriers.

aggressively along these routes, a large North American hub-and-spoke system is critical. Although U.S. and Canadian carriers possess such hubs, a North American hub is not feasible for Hong Kong's airlines. As a result, Cathay Pacific has only limited opportunities to profitably expand in the North American market, and limits its U.S.-bound freighter service to a few flights per week.

North American carriers also have the advantage of being able to use Tokyo's Narita Airport as an "offshore" hub. No comparable facility is available for Asian airlines to facilitate their expansion into North America (Westlake, 1992). Many analysts believe that local airlines will be unable to participate extensively in North American markets until they follow the lead of Singapore Airlines and enter a marketing alliance or acquire an equity stake in a North American or European carrier. By protecting incumbent carriers, however, restrictive air service agreements discourage this type of initiative.[5]

(3) Fostering External Benefits

Some defenders of the restrictive bilateral policy believe that protecting local producers from foreign competitors is justified because local carriers provide large external benefits to the regional economy. Local airlines are said to provide benefits that "spill over" into other sectors of the Hong Kong economy, such as the labor market, supplier services, and local government. Undoubtedly, local carriers may be associated with some external benefits, but these benefits constitute a dubious defense of the restrictive aviation policies.

Consider the external benefits with respect to employment. While restrictive policies may protect jobs at incumbent carriers, these jobs are generally offset by reduced employment among foreign airlines,

---

5. For a more thorough discussion of how economies of scope affect international air carriers, see Ethan Weismann, *Trade in Services and Imperfect Competition*, Kluwer Academic Publishers, Boston, 1990.

which would also rely on Hong Kong citizens to support their operations. According to the Hong Kong Census, foreign airlines offer comparable compensation packages to employees (Census and Statistics Department, 1992). Moreover, considering that unemployment is virtually non-existent among skilled workers in Hong Kong, and that workers often have attractive alternatives, it must be remembered that there are high opportunity costs associated with employment in the aviation sector. One local company, HAECO, for example, faces such severe shortages that it is importing staff from the United Kingdom and expects to use personnel trained in mainland China. Thus, while benefits from additional employment by local air companies are positive, they constitute only a small fraction of the total wages paid — particularly for clerical and white-collar jobs where labor shortages are most severe.

Some believe that an enlarged market share by foreign airlines would render South China vulnerable to the service embargoes, service cuts, or price increases of foreign airlines or governments. But advocates of this view fail to recognize that air cargo services are merely a derived demand; demand for such services is related to the demand for other products. South China's export-driven economy would be exposed to little additional risk in foreign diplomacy if foreign carriers transported a larger share of its exports. In fact, a more liberal aviation policy could reduce the region's economic vulnerability by ushering in a diversified, regional hub at Chek Lap Kok. This would render the region less dependent on goods moving between Guangdong Province and the West, improving the region's ability to withstand a trade dispute between the United States and China. Similarly, by attracting a more diverse mix of carriers, the Provisional Airport Authority would develop a more stable revenue base and would be able to retire airport debt more quickly, improving the financial position of the future Special Administrative Region government.

(4) Stabilizing Prices

The existing bilateral process is believed by some to be necessary to stabilize prices. Some officials maintain that unregulated air markets are inherently volatile, characterized by excessive price cutting, bankruptcies, and service disruptions. Because they limit capacity, restrictive air service agreements are seen as a way of bolstering prices, thus encouraging carriers to make long-range investments in Hong Kong. Some authorities in Hong Kong fear that the territory's airline industry would be unable to modernize or expand profitably in a more competitive environment.

This is a weak argument. By denying carriers the flexibility they need to efficiently utilize their aircraft, existing bilateral treaties sometime have the opposite effect: they destabilize prices by inhibiting carriers from building hub systems that could improve the utilization of aircraft inventory. Moreover, evidence suggests that erecting entry barriers to promote price stability results in higher costs to shippers and consumers (Morrison and Winston, 1986, 1990). Other countries, including Australia, Canada, China, and those in the European Economic Community, recognize that the associated gains from more liberal air policies greatly exceed any losses associated with price instability.

The favorable experiences of Hong Kong's neighbors, such as South Korea, Taiwan, Malaysia, and Singapore, which have adopted more liberal policies, show that erecting entry barriers to enhance price stability is unnecessary. These countries do not experience excessive price cutting. On the contrary, their two leading airlines, Korean Air and Singapore Airlines, have reported profits even greater than those of Cathay Pacific Airlines. One reason that cargo prices are so stable is the high opportunity costs of carrying "belly" cargo. When facing limitations on an aircraft's weight at departure, carriers are understandably reluctant to displace passenger traffic for lower-yielding cargo traffic.

(5) *Bargaining for Reciprocal Benefits*

Finally, although many officials concede that Hong Kong would benefit from fewer entry barriers, some question the desirability of a unilateral action. After all, they maintain, if other countries are willing to give Hong Kong new aviation opportunities in return for the right to carry cargo from the territory, why should not Hong Kong pursue these opportunities?

As long as the governments of other nations restrict access of Hong Kong carriers, there may be instances when Hong Kong will have good reason to expect something in return for its concessions.[6] An occasional dispute is believed to be a reasonable price to pay for additional traffic rights for Hong Kong's carriers. However, this argument has two serious problems as a defense of the existing bilateral approach.

First, as discussed earlier, the bilateral policy subjects a huge segment of the South China economy to an awkward, unpredictable, and politicized process. This not only places upward pressure on prices, it amplifies the risks of doing business in the South China region. There is growing evidence that bilateral negotiations could soon be linked with trade issues, such as the enforcement of export quotas where Hong Kong's bargaining position is extremely weak. This would increase the vulnerability of air cargo shippers to a whole new category of trade disputes. The American Chamber of Commerce has already warned that the current negotiating strategy, with its emphasis on the "imbalance" in air services between Hong Kong and the United States, may be destined to lead to an even more serious and costly trade dispute — an outcome that would be devastating to South China's economy.

6. According to one member of Hong Kong's Air Services Negotiating Unit, the group directly responsible for all agreements, this is a common strategy in its negotiations. The government looks for an equal balance of exchange in all negotiations (Yue, 1992). The Hong Kong Chamber of Commerce supports the assumption that bilateral negotiations should be used to their full potential in situations where the colony is negotiating from a position of strength, as they are in banking, communications, and transportation services. Where Hong Kong is only a relatively small player, such as in the textiles market, the Chamber believes that Hong Kong should pursue a multilateral process, pooling its resources with other countries toward a collective goal. In these situations, a multilateral policy is seen as a way to enhance Hong Kong's bargaining position and lower the risk of antagonizing neighboring countries.

Second, there is good reason to believe that the government is not actually using the bilateral process to gain concessions from foreign governments. In negotiations with the United States, for example, local officials concede that the most stringent demand by Hong Kong negotiators — for cabotage rights, or the right to serve two cities within the United States — is not worth as much to local carriers as is commonly believed. Demanding cabotage rights in the U.S. may be merely a tactic to perpetuate the stalemate that is protecting the market share of Hong Kong carriers, most notably Cathay Pacific. Other local officials maintain that the U.S. government is incapable of offering any concession that would satisfy the territory's requirement of "equal exchange" of traffic rights. Considering the Hong Kong government's unwillingness to take steps to break the impasse, its continuation seems inevitable, effectively halting the growth of many express cargo services into South China.

As the above analysis shows, many are mistaken in their belief that the region's economic interests are best served through restrictive bilateral treaties. Although the Hong Kong government may occasionally succeed in pressing foreign governments to grant additional traffic rights, local businesses must not rely on current bargaining strategy, which often has little to do with this worthy goal.

3. Conclusion

This study illustrates why Hong Kong must overhaul its policies toward air cargo and sweep away the outmoded, anti-competitive practices that are inhibiting regional growth. Four findings exemplify Chek Lap Kok's potential.

- The rapid industrialization of South China requires a dynamic and resourceful air cargo industry at Chek Lap Kok. Total air cargo tonnage is expected to grow by 700 percent by 2030, requiring risk-taking and innovation throughout the industry. As Guangdong Province expands to become one of the world's premier manufacturing districts, Hong Kong must give air cargo providers enough flexibility for expansion and the improvement of services. Decisive action is needed to meet the challenges posed by new airports being constructed throughout Asia.

- Hong Kong has an opportunity to vastly improve its local air cargo services by fostering the development of an express cargo hub at Chek Lap Kok. Express cargo carriers providing overnight, door-to-door service, already an integral part of North American and European transportation systems, soon will become an integral part of Asia's air cargo system. The development of Chek Lap Kok as an express hub would stimulate competition and generate new aeronautical revenues, directly benefiting the region by as much as HK$571 million annually. This hub would be a linchpin to the growth and prosperity of the entire South China region.
- The Provisional Airport Authority must establish a competitive market for terminal services at Chek Lap Kok to pave the way for a major hub operation. The existing terminal arrangement, which relies on the services of a regulated monopoly, cannot be expected to accommodate the complex, specialized needs of cargo hub operators. Airlines must be empowered to choose terminal operators and intervene in the terminal process to enhance product differentiation and quality control.

Under the suggested proposal, the Provisional Airport Authority would award licenses to two terminal operators at Chek Lap Kok (or three operators if additional land can be made available) and charge each operator a flat franchise fee annually. One terminal would be operated directly by express airlines and offer dedicated facilities for express cargo. Rates for these services would be negotiated freely between terminal operators and airlines, just as they are under the duopoly system at Singapore's Changi Airport.

- Finally, the Economic Services Branch must take steps to remove all-cargo flights from the existing bilateral negotiating process, which is currently dominated by passenger-related concerns. The proposal calls for the Branch to unilaterally offer a limited number of fifth freedom rights to foreign carriers serving Kai Tak Airport with all-cargo flights. To assure that regulatory and political issues do not impede hub development at Chek Lap Kok, the proposal also calls for an offer of unlimited traffic rights for all-cargo flights following the new airport's opening. In addition, it calls for the Air Transport

Licensing Authority to take action by authorizing other local carriers to join Cathay Pacific in serving important Asian destinations. Over the long term, Hong Kong is urged to support efforts to move all air cargo negotiations to a multilateral process, such as the General Agreement on Tariffs and Trade. Taking these steps will provide a solid foundation for continued economic growth and a vital and prosperous Chek Lap Kok enterprise.

Appendix

The regression model examines cargo prices in 125 Asian city pairs (Table 1). All prices are converted into Hong Kong dollars and represent prices for air cargo shipments weighing 45 kilograms or less (prices for heavier movements are not considered). The sample is limited to prices for air cargo shipments originating in six Asian cities, Bangkok, Hong Kong, Kuala Lumpur, Manila, Singapore, and Taiwan. For example, the sample includes the price of shipping a 45-kilogram parcel from Hong Kong to Frankfurt (HK$62.95 per kilogram), but ignores the price of shipping a similar shipment from Frankfurt to Hong Kong (HK$32.50 per kilogram), after adjusting for flight distance and market size.

The results show that prices rise nonlinearly with flight distance and fall with the levels of cargo volume (Table 2). This latter finding may be due to the fact that busy routes tend to be competitive, and to be served with larger, more efficient aircraft. (This coefficient is

Table 1. Model Description

Dependent Variable	
Price	Price of air cargo service for shipments originating in various Asian cities and weighing less than 45 kilograms, measured in Hong Kong dollars per kilogram.
Independent Variable	
Distance	Distance between origin and destination, measured in miles.
Distsq	Square of distance between origin and destination, measured in miles.
Volume	Annual volume of air cargo between the origin and destination, expressed as a log of annual tonnage.
HongKong	Dummy variable assuming a value of one for services originating in Hong Kong.

not statistically significant.) A dummy variable designating prices applicable to shippers in Hong Kong has a positive, statistically significant coefficient. Other versions of this model, such as a log-linear specification, produce a similar result.

Table 2. Regression Model Results

Dependent Variable		Price per kilogram (in HK dollars)
Sample size		121
Degrees of freedom		116
R^2		0.77
	Coefficient	T Statistic
Constant	4.30	0.4
Distance	0.013	13.2*
Distsq	–0.00000076	6.9*
Volume	–0.77	1.25
Hong Kong	4.31	1.71*

* Statistically significant at .95 level (one tailed test).

Bibliography

1. *Air Cargo Guide* (1993). Official Airline Guides, Oak Brook, Illinois, Volume 37, No. 1, January.
2. Bailey, Elizabeth David R. Graham and Daniel P., Kaplan (1985). *Deregulating the Airlines*. MIT Press, Cambridge, Mass.
3. Bangsberg, P.T. (1992). "Analysts Upbeat about Airport in Hong Kong Despite Deadlock." *Journal of Commerce*, 31 July.
4. ——— (1992). "Modificiations in Hong Kong Airport Vindicate Earlier Protests, China Says." *Journal of Commerce*, 19 August.
5. Bowring, Phillip (1992a). "Cathay Flies the Friendship Skies." Unpublished manuscript.
6. ——— (1992b). "Controversy at Chek Lap Kok." Unpublished manuscript.
7. Carlton, Dennis W., William Landes, and Richard Posner (1980). "Benefits and Costs of Airline Mergers: A Case Study." *Bell Journal of Economics*, Spring.
8. Cathay Pacific Airlines (1992). Letter dated 2 January.
9. Census and Statistics Department, Transport and Services Statistics Section (1990). *Survey of Transport & Related Services.* Government Printer, Hong Kong.
10. Dittler, Allan (1992). "Express Carriers Took-off after Deregulation." *Air Cargo World*, March.
11. *Economist* (1992). "Another Chinese Take-off." 19 December.
12. *Executive* (1992). "Should Air Cargo Handling Be a Monopoly Business?" December, p. 34.
13. *Executive Express: Communication to Customers from DHL* (1993). "New Regional Hub Opens." January.
14. Federal Express Airlines (1993). "Federal Express Corporate

Highlights."

15. *Fortune* (1992). "Bracing for Japan's Hot New Strategy." 21 September, pp. 62–74.
16. Gellman Research Associates (1990). *A Study of the Benefits to the Hong Kong Economy from Increased Air Cargo Capacity in Inter-Asia Markets*. Philadelphia.
17. Gish, Judy (1991). "Japan's Other Airlines." *Air Cargo World*, February, p. 34.
18. Godfrey, P. (1991). "Fare Increase Warning over Kai Tak Fees." *South China Morning*, 5 November, p. 3.
19. Hasting, Phillip (1991). "Cathay Expands Cargo Network." *Air Commerce*.
20. Hong Kong Air Cargo Terminals Limited (1992). *HACTL's Proposal for an Express Cargo Facility at Chek Lap Kok Airport*. Mimeo.
21. *Hong Kong Standard* (1989). "HAECO Begins to Battle Staff Shortage Problems." 7 August.
22. Horne, L. (1992). "IATA Chief Hits out over High Airport Charge." *South China Morning Post*, 9 July.
23. *IATA Member Statistics* (1991). International Air Transport Association, Montreal.
24. Johnson, Richard (1985). "Networking and Market Entry in the Airline Industry." *Journal of Transport Economics*, September.
25. Ko, K. (1991). "HACTL Seeks 28.9pc Rise in Handling Rates." *South China Morning Post*, 16 November.
26. Krugman, Paul R. (1987). "Is Free Trade Passe?" *Journal of Economic Perspectives*, Fall, pp. 131–44.
27. Kwong, Kai-sun (1988). *Toward Open Skies and Uncongested Airport: An Opportunity for Hong Kong*. Hong Kong Centre for Economic Research and The Chinese University Press, Hong Kong.

28. Lieberthan, Kenneth (1992). "Hong Kong Scenarios." *The China Business Review*. September.

29. Linn, Eugene (1992). "Hong Kong Cargo Rises to New Heights." *Air Cargo World*, October.

30. Mama, Hormuz (1992). "Expansion Plans for Changi Airport." *Airport Forum*, January.

31. Martin, Graham (1991). "Airlines and Nations Barter Their Bilaterals." *Air Cargo World*. November.

32. McKee, Charles D., Jr. (1991). "Air Cargo Takes Off." *China Business Review*. September.

33. Miners, Norman (1991). *The Government and Politics of Hong Kong*. Oxford University Press, New York.

34. Morrison, Steven A. and Winston, Clifford (1986). *The Economic Effects of Airline Deregulation.* Brookings Institution, Washington, D.C.

35. ——— (1987). "Empirical Implications of the Contestability Hypothesis." *Journal of Law and Economics*, Spring.

36. ——— (1990). "The Dynamics of Airline Pricing and Competition." *American Economic Review*, May.

37. *New Airport Master Plan: Executive Summary* (1992). Provisional Airport Authority, Hong Kong.

38. Page, Paul (1993). "TNT Starts First Intra-Asia Express Network." *Traffic World,* 5 April.

39. *Payload Asia* (1992). "SATS Leads the Way." February 1992, p. 24.

40. Director of Civil Aviation (1992). *Report on Civil Aviation Hong Kong: 1990–91*. Government Printer, Hong Kong.

41. Schano, Richard (1992). "Taiwan Develops CKS Airport into Asian Transportation Center." *Air Cargo World*, January.

42. Schwieterman, Joseph P. (1992) "Stormy Skies: Pricing Lessons for America's Airlines. *USA Today Monthly*, September.

43. Schwieterman, Joseph P. (1993) "Express Air Cargo in the Pacific Rim: An Evaluation of Prospective Hub Sites." Working paper, Public Services Program, DePaul University, Chicago, Illinois.

44. Scott, Bruce (1990). "Creating Comparative Advantage." In *International Economics and International Economic Policy: A Reader*, Philip King (ed.). McGraw Hill, New York.

45. Selwitz, Robert (1991). "Cathay Committed to Freighters." *Air Cargo World*, January.

46. *Shippers Today* (1992). "Air Hong Kong Wins Global Rights." May.

47. ——— (1992a). "Pearl River Delta Region — Hong Kong's Goldmine." January.

48. ——— (1992b). "US Gets Tough with China." March.

49. ——— (1992c). "China's Consumer Market Opens Up." May.

50. ——— (1992d). "New Challenges to Hong Kong Industry." July.

51. ——— (1992e). "Port & Airport Developments of the New Tigers." July.

52. ——— (1992f). "Tougher Battle for Asian Freight Forwarders." March.

53. ——— (1992g). "Hong Kong Is China's Window to the World." November.

54. ——— (1993). "Air Freight Statistics." March.

55. Sung, Yun-Wing (1991). *The China-Hong Kong Connection: The Key to China's Open-Door Policy*. Cambridge University Press, Cambridge, U.K.

56. *TACT Rates: North America* (1992). The Air Cargo Tariff, Utrecht, Netherlands. No. 92, July.

57. *TACT Rates: Worldwide* (1992). The Air Cargo Tariff, Utrecht, Netherlands. No. 90, July.

58. Tong, Davia and Gargo Cheung (1991). "Launching PADS." *The*

China Business Review. May.

59. Weismann, Ethan (1990). *Trade in Services and Imperfect Competition*. Kluwer Academic Publishers, Boston.
60. Westlake, Michael (1991). "Profit Formation: Asia's Aviation Twins Exhibit Key Differences." *Far Eastern Economic Review*, 27 June.
61. ——— (1992). "Freedom to Fly: Hongkong under Pressure from US for More Access." *Far Eastern Economic Review*, 12 March.
62. ——— (1992a). "Opening up the Skies: Asian Carriers Look to Era of Fewer Flying Restrictions." *Far Eastern Economic Review*, 25 July.
63. ——— (1992b). "Airport Blues: Government Fights Myth of Spiralling Costs." *Far Eastern Economic Review*, 2 July.
64. Wong, Richard (1992). "Competition in Container Terminals." HKCER Letters: A Publication of the Hong Kong Centre for Economic Research, September.
65. Yue, S.Y. (1992). "Air Services Pacts Face More Delay." *South China Morning Post*, July 31.

Index